HIGHLAND SUMMER

Highland Summer

SETON GORDON, C.B.E., F.Z.S.

Illustrated by
JEANNE CROSS and STUART HARRISON

CASSELL · LONDON

CASSELL & COMPANY LTD
35 Red Lion Square, London, WC1
Sydney, Auckland
Toronto, Johannesburg

First published 1971

I.S.B.N. 0 304 93775 4

Printed in Great Britain
by Ebenezer Baylis and Son Ltd
The Trinity Press, Worcester, and London
F.471

Many books have been written on the Highlands and Islands of Scotland. Perhaps the most outstanding account of the way of life in the Outer Hebrides in the days when I first knew them is in a book, *A School in South Uist*, published, through the efforts of John Lorne Campbell of Canna, by Routledge and Kegan Paul comparatively recently. The author is F. G. Rea, a Birmingham man who, with no knowledge of Scotland or its Western Isles, took up his duties as head teacher of a school on the Island of South Uist on 2 January in the year 1890. This book in a unique manner brings before the reader the life of the Gaelic-speaking people of this romantic island at that time. The writer found himself on an island where most people understood little or no English, and which to him was a foreign land, but surmounted his difficulties and gradually came to know and love the island in a unique way.

The Highlands are swiftly changing in character. In many districts the Gaelic language survives only in the place-names; in others it is spoken only by the older generation, and indeed there are now few districts where Gaelic is the language of the young generation. In old days the family and its neighbours gathered round a peat fire on a winter's evening and held a social gathering or Ceilidh, where tales of the past were recited and songs were sung. The company now sit silent beside a television screen, or listen on their wireless set to the latest news bulletin from a materialistic world. This is the day of the tourist, and of the litter which he leaves behind him. But there are still Highland areas which have not felt the heavy hand of 'progress', and in this book I have endeavoured to convey to the reader the abiding charm of hill and glen and of the wild creatures which have their home here.

There are chapters on the Isle of Skye, and on the high Cairngorms in 'Highland Summer', in which I have described the source of the River Dee on the Braeriach plateau, where the climber reaches the nearest approach to Arctic conditions in Scotland. The Dee, rising here at 4,000 feet above the sea, has the highest source of any British river. I have known that distinguished river for many years; one of my earliest memories is of sliding on its frozen surface on a deep salmon pool and seeing the salmon, safe from the hardy angler, swimming unafraid beneath me. That was during the Arctic winter of 1894–5, and much water has flowed through the river since then.

Some of the chapters in the book have already appeared in print. My special thanks are due to the Editors of *The Times, The Field, The Scotsman,* and *Country Life* for permission to use articles. I should like to thank, also, the Editors of two Scottish magazines, namely *Scotland's Magazine,* and *The Scots Magazine,* the latter a paper of such old standing that one can read in a back number a contemporary account of the landing of Bonnie Prince Charlie in the year 1745.

SETON GORDON

Duntuilm, Isle of Skye
March 1971

Contents

Contents

Highland Summer

It was a quarter to five on a cloudless morning in late July. As I stood at my bedroom window in the Castle of Invercauld on the River Dee near Braemar I saw the swifts which nest in the tower fly out into the cold, almost frosty air and climb towards the Lion's Face and its rocks, already a dull gold in the warmth of the rising sun. A quick breakfast and we were off in my friend's Land-Rover on the fifteen-mile drive to The Derry. Braemar village, a hive of activity at this summer season, was still asleep; on Beinn a' Bhuird, high above it, the sun shone on the great snowfield known locally as The Laird of Invercauld's Table-cloth. In Glen Lui there were red deer and, when we arrived at Lui Beag—the only cottage in this lovely glen—we found that energetic deerstalker Bob Scott already preparing his porridge to fortify himself for a long day on the river.

As we set out on our walk, for the first five miles through the Lairig Ghru Pass, we soon realized that the snowfields on the Cairngorms were unusually large that summer. Ahead of us, Monadh Mór on the west horizon held an extensive snow-wreath in its east corrie, and there were also 'pockets' of snow on remote Beinn Bhrodain. Close to us, on the heathery slope of Carn Crom, the historic Scots fir, known as The Tree of Gold, cast its long shadow across the hill slope. This tree must be centuries old, for native Scots firs, survivors of the ancient Caledonian Forest, grow slowly. I have known this tree (I write in 1970) for almost seventy years, yet I see no change in its height or foliage, although some of its neighbours have died and stand naked, with stems almost as white as snow. In olden times cattle raiders from Lochaber, on their way to despoil the rich cattle-rearing lands of the east, are said to have sheltered, or perhaps hidden, near here and the place-name, Preas nam Meirleach, survives, its English translation being The Robbers' Thicket. The old hill track to the west on which we walked crosses the *Mam* or Low Shoulder of the hill Carn a' Mhaim and near its fourth and only milestone from Derry Lodge the walker arrives in sight of the highest reaches of Glen Dee and sees great hills rise before him. The Devil's Point and Cairntoul tower from

I

the west bank of the river and Ben MacDhui from the east. The long ridge of Braeriach forms the north-west horizon. The track now descends 200 feet to the River Dee, where a footbridge now spans the river, and a path leads to the Corrour Bothy. This strong 'bothan' or bothy, built a hundred years ago as a deer watcher's dwelling, is now perhaps the only bothy remaining on the Cairngorm Hills; it has been repaired by the Cairngorm Club and is now popular with mountaineers. Strangely enough, it was empty when we looked in, although a pair of black-headed gulls, encouraged no doubt by frequent scraps of food, were hopefully awaiting us.

This bothy has pleasant memories for me. I recall summers here before the first world war. About 1910 John McIntosh, known locally as The Piper, was deer watcher here. He was a strong, upright man, of distinguished appearance, and was an excellent piper. Many a summer evening and night I spent with him here; one very dark night I was actually guided to the bothy by his playing. Like the deer stalkers at Lui Beag and The Derry he was a Gaelic speaker and enjoyed reading the Gaelic pieces in the *Oban Times*. That newspaper, printed in Oban far west of the Cairngorms, was passed by hand, with respect and even veneration, from one stalker to another in the Braemar area. In those days Corrour Bothy had a box bed. The comfortable mattress from this bed was laid on the floor for the guest, who slept in the warmth of a fire of bog fir and peat. There were few climbers on the hills in those days and when I tuned my pipes outside the bothy door the red deer used to approach and listen; they were obviously excited by the stirring notes of the Highland bagpipe.

Our destination on this July morning was far beyond Corrour Bothy; we left it and its warden gulls and climbed the steep slope of the corrie known as Coire Odhar, or Corrour in its anglicized form. We walked beside a clear burn where the starry saxifrage was in flower and at 3,000 feet above sea level arrived at the small plateau of the Devil's Point where a few late flowers of the Alpine azalea opened small pink china-like petals. The sun was warm as we climbed a more gradual grassy slope, where winter snowfields still lingered, to granite screes near the summit of Cairntoul (4,241 feet) and lunched at an ice-cold spring at Clais an t-Sabhail, in English, The Hollow of the Barn. I spent many days and nights here before the first war watching a cock snow-bunting: himself beautiful, he had an exceptionally loud and beautiful song. The rock which was his main singing post is still there but it is many a year since the snow-bunting nested here. On a hot summer day this small, handsome black-and-white bird used to refresh himself by running over a snowfield, using his head as a miniature snow-plough.

After lunch we toiled across granite screes to look into the deep chasm of Garbh Choire Mór, in English, The Great Rough Corrie, and its snowbed, which has melted only twice in the last sixty years. We noticed a pair of ptarmigan dozing in the sun near us. We climbed to the west top of Braeriach and stood at a height of 4,100 feet, at the margin of a broad plateau. This gives a unique view of the Scottish Highlands, near and far. We saw the distant hill of Morven in Caithness on the northern horizon, Ben Nevis (Scotland's highest hill) and Ben Alder far westward, and even Ben Dorain and the hills of the Blackmount Forest in Argyll. One of the most celebrated songs of the Gaelic poet, Duncan Ban Macintyre, is one in 'Praise of Ben Dorain'. The music to which this song is sung is in the form of a Piobaireachd, the classical music of the Highland bagpipe. On the plateau where we stood are the Wells of Dee. Here, at 4,000 feet above the distant North Sea or the equally distant Atlantic Ocean, the River Dee, which flows past the Queen's castle at Balmoral, has its lofty birth-place. The rays of the July sun beat fiercely upon us; never have the waters of the Wells been more appreciated; and were enjoyed the more when drunk from the ancient silver Highland cup carried by my friend.

Here, almost a thousand feet above the heather-line, one is on the roof of the Scottish Highlands and the vegetation may be compared to the tundra of the Arctic. It is also, for a short season, a natural rock-garden of great beauty where many acres of the delightful cushion pink (*Silene acaulis*) flower. The plant lover is indeed fortunate if his summer visit to the plateau should coincide with the flowering of this plant. In the year 1960 my wife and I were here on June 20 when the whole plateau was rose-tinted, and towards sunset the sight was one that could never be forgotten. On the present expedition, therefore, five weeks later, I expected to find the plants already in seed. To my surprise, few of these cushion pink plants were even in flower. Many were in bud, but many more had scarcely begun to grow, and it could be seen that the winter snow-cover had only recently melted. The season of summer at this elevation varies greatly; indeed, on a visit as long ago as 1907 I found the young Dee here entirely invisible beneath the drifted snow of a July blizzard.

Later that afternoon we crossed the plateau, near a white quartz memorial stone, and looked down on to Loch Eanaich, home of the red-bellied char, beyond which rose darkly the precipitous slopes of Sgoran Dubh. Beyond the old fir forest of Rothiemurchus flowed the River Spey, a silver ribbon in the westering sun. In the days of steam the whistle of a train at Aviemore station on the Spey could be heard on Braeriach plateau, ten miles distant.

It was evening when we set out on our long return walk to The Derry in Mar Forest. Our way took us across the deep snowfield near the head of Horseman's Corrie, a corrie which received its name from an enthusiastic tenant of Glen Feshie deer forest many years ago. Descending an easy slope we passed close to Loch nan Stuirteag, loch of the black-headed gulls, its water almost 3,000 feet above the sea. Sandpipers sing and nest here, but no black-headed gulls have nested in my time. In recent years, however, a colony of common gulls have nested on its small island and this summer evening we saw young gulls swimming on the calm water. We now descended into deep and dark Glen Giusachan, disturbing a hen ptarmigan brooding closely on a late hatch of seven nestlings. She slipped away silently and they remained almost motionless, a fluffy and contented family.

In Glen Giusachan we were on the traditional hunting ground of the Feinne or Fingalians. These Celtic heroes, who lived before the birth of Christ, are still commemorated in Highland place-names. The name of a deep corrie above the glen is Coire Cath nam Fiann, Corrie of the Battle of the Fingalians. Near it rises Beinn Bhrodain, and this hill, like Loch Bhrodain in Gaick Forest, may have associations with the jet-black demon hound named Brodain who was owned by a mythical hunter, perhaps one of the same heroic band. Glen Giusachan is a deceptively long glen, especially after a walk of many hours; as we traversed it the shadows were slowly lengthening and the great snowfield on Monadh Mór, which we had seen in bright sunshine early that morning, now was in blue shadow.

Glen Giusachan is now treeless, but we passed, at 2,400 feet above sea level, the peat-preserved roots of a noble Scots fir, an outpost of the ancient forest which gave the glen its name, Glen of the Fir Trees.

During the hours we had spent on the high hills the River Dee had risen because of the melting snowfields. We heard the river music as we passed a gigantic boulder precariously deposited by a glacier thousands of years ago on a heathery knoll, and, at nine o'clock in the evening, reached the River Dee. The sun, low in the north-west sky, still shone as we searched for a crossing place, for we had reached the river far below the foot-bridge we had used in the

morning. The agitated flutings of a bird mingled with the roar of a formidable rushing stream. At last we were across, but had now to climb at least 200 feet to reach the path on the shoulder on Carn a' Mhaim, passing on our climb Clais a' Mhadadh, Hollow of the Wolf, the lair of one of the last wolves in the Highlands of Scotland. There was still sufficient daylight to follow this path when, an hour before midnight, we saw ahead of us the light in Bob Scott's cottage, which we had left seventeen hours before. There was little time for a talk here, and the Land-Rover was soon carrying us, a skilled driver at the wheel, over the rough road to the Linn of Dee. After we had crossed the Linn with its deep, salmon-crowded pools the road was good, but it was half an hour after midnight, as afterglow was merging with sunrise, before we saw the welcoming lights of the Castle of Invercauld.

A Skye Fortress Awaiting Completion

On the north wing of the Isle of Skye a gaunt castle nearly three hundred years old stands at the very edge of the sea. It is invisible from the road and few of the many visitors to Skye have seen it. This strange, imposing building is Caisteal Huisdein, in English Hugh's Castle, and the beauty and symmetry of its weathered walls are still evident. Hugh was a close relative of the chief of the MacDonalds. Huisdein is the Gaelic name for Hugh, and his full Gaelic name was Huisdein MacGillespic Chleirich, in English, Hugh, Son of Gillespic the Writer. His record was dark, ruthless, dishonest. He longed for more power and plotted against his chief. His boat or galley, named *An Ealadh*, 'The Swan', was usually moored at Cuidreach, on the same shore a couple of miles to the north. The bay where it was anchored is still known in the district as Pol na h-Ealaidh, Pool of the Swan.

Not without reason, Hugh mistrusted his fellow men. Caisteal Huisdein was never actually completed but was designed to offer a formidable defence. The lower part of the building was to be without windows, and it can still be seen that the only doorway or entrance is approximately nine feet above the ground. Entrance was therefore impossible except by a ladder, which could be drawn up and kept inside the building when not in use. The castle is built on the very edge of the cliff and therefore could not be surrounded by hostile attack. When the building was nearing completion Hugh decided to invite his chief to a banquet, and to have him murdered at the end of the feast. He entered into correspondence with one named Martin, who was to carry out the murder.

Now came Hugh's act of extreme carelessness, which cost him his life. He wrote a letter to his chief at Duntuilm Castle, inviting him to the 'house warming', and another to Martin with careful instructions on how the chief should be killed. Envelopes had not then been invented, as we now know them, but each letter was placed in its covering and sent by messenger. What happened showed that either Hugh had been incredibly careless, or the messengers themselves had acted treacherously. This will never be known, but the MacDonald chief received the letter intended for Martin. That moment must have

7

been one of high drama. The chief acted promptly. He sent the ancestor of the MacDonalds of Kingsburgh, whose patronymic was Domhnall MacIain ic Sheumais (Donald Son of Iain, Son of James) and who was the best swordsman in Skye, to Cuidreach to apprehend Hugh and bring him, alive or dead, to Duntuilm Castle. Hugh escaped with difficulty but succeeded in boarding his galley and immediately set sail for North Uist across the Minch. He was followed, and was captured there after withstanding a siege on the small fortified island of a freshwater loch. Securely bound, he was brought back to the chief's landing place at Duntuilm Castle, where the shelter excavated for the chief's galleys is still to be seen. He was imprisoned in the dungeon and a little later a large portion of salt beef was lowered to him. He was ravenous for he had been without food since his capture. Later, tormented by thirst, he called loudly for water. A pewter jug was lowered and he greedily seized it, only to find it empty. He died an unpleasant death.

Huisdein or Hugh was a man of great size and strength. His skull and thigh bones were for centuries preserved beside a window of Kilmuir Church, three miles south of Duntuilm until, in 1827, they were given burial.

The walls of Caisteal Huisdein are a lasting memorial to those who built them. When seen from a distance the building might well be an outcrop of the cliff itself, so firm and enduring does it seem. During the days of mid-October, when the scent of the bog myrtle is even more aromatic and stronger than at mid-summer, the white wings of passing whooper swans, weary after their long flight from Iceland, move at deceptive speed low over the castle. Almost completed by Huisdein, it has remained his memorial through subsequent centuries.

Later in the autumn great northern divers, large and majestic birds, may almost daily be watched fishing in the sea below the castle. These expert fishermen, almost as large as geese, are able to remain submerged longer than either cormorant or shag. Fishermen believed this diver to be incapable of flight, and that early each summer it swam the eight hundred miles from Scottish waters to Iceland to nest, in autumn swimming back to Scottish waters where the winter was less severe. It is true this large diver is rarely seen in flight, but it can, if necessary, fly fast and far; it is possible, however, that the migration may indeed be made partly by swimming. There have been rumours from time to time of a great northern diver's nest and eggs in the north of Scotland, but no confirmation of this has ever been obtained. The birds indeed sometimes remain until mid-June in Scottish waters and by this time have grown their handsome summer plumage. The black guillemot, a bird which in autumn and winter has more white than black in its plumage, is often seen below Caisteal Huisdein. Like the great northern diver, it finds most of its food below the surface, and travels far unseen close to the ocean's floor as it hunts small fish.

When the ebbing tides leaves clear rock-pools with their crowded population of barnacles, attractive purple sandpipers, autumn and winter visitors to the Isle of Skye from Greenland, are sometimes seen in small parties. Their bills are strong and, almost alone among shore-feeding birds, they are able to feed on barnacles. It was pleasant to see them one sunny afternoon as they bathed joyfully in the ice-cold water of a pool, throwing sparkling spray over themselves, and one another, with impetuous beating of their dark wings as they stood thigh-deep. They were indifferent both to the ravens which sailed high along the coast, uttering strong far-carrying croaking cries as they passed, and to a buzzard that spiralled idly, with high-pitched querulous mewing, on eddies of ocean wind.

The fugitive Prince Charles Edward Stuart, disguised in woman's clothes, in the year 1746 must have passed close to Caisteal Huisdein on his anxious walk from Mugstot, where he was landed in great secrecy, to the friendly house of Kingsburgh. A little later, when Samuel Johnson and his friend Boswell stayed at Kingsburgh House with Flora MacDonald and her husband, they may have been taken to see the castle. It is evident that the walls of the castle have been built by master craftsmen. Strong and abiding, they will remain through the centuries that are to come, a memorial of a grim figure of an earlier age when a Highland Chief had the power of life and death in his hands.

Ebb and Flow of Highland Bird Life

Looking back over half a century, I see many changes in Highland wild life. Perhaps the most pleasing is the return of the osprey. It would really be more correct to say that the osprey has been established as a new nesting species in Scotland, because it is improbable that any descendants of the old Highland ospreys are still alive. Protection at their nesting sites in the north of Scandinavia has resulted in the increase of the ospreys in that region. Strathspey is on the migration line of Scandinavian ospreys, which are of necessity migrants because of the freezing of their homeland lakes in winter.

A pair of young Scandinavian ospreys, returning for their first nesting, may have been attracted by the friendly appearance of the lochs and pine forests of the Spey, and may have decided to end their northern migration and make their nest here. That in itself was a great event, but it is unfortunately true that any bird as rare, and as conspicuous, as the osprey has little chance of establishing itself in Britain unless it is given the most careful protection. As I write, the Royal Society for the Protection of Birds has given this pair of ospreys such thorough protection that each year for ten summers they have usually reared their young successfully. Much of the credit of 'Operation Ospreys' has been due to the tireless enthusiasm of Mr George Waterston.

Fifty years ago there was a large stock of ptarmigan on the Cairngorms and on the White Mounth, as the Lochnagar massif is sometimes named. The stock of these attractive birds has since then varied from season to season, but is now much smaller than it was around, let us say, the years 1922–3. It was at this time that 'grouse disease' thinned the stock, and it is still far below earlier numbers.

When the stock of ptarmigan is plentiful, the cocks have a habit of leaving the hens to care for the chicks after the eggs hatch, and of joining other cocks similarly situated. These gatherings of cock ptarmigan I used to see on the summit plateau of Braeriach in the nineteen-twenties when, from mid-June until late in the month, or early in July, their white wings as they suddenly rose were an attractive sight. This separation from their families was only temporary, and the cocks returned to their broods when the young were feathered. I do not think the stock of ptarmigan is sufficiently large for this habit to be seen anywhere in Scotland at the present day.

Another change in the bird life of the Cairngorms is in the habits of the common gull and the black-headed gull. The common gull is now nesting on two of the high lochs where previously it was unknown. One of these is Loch Etchachan, 3,100 feet above sea level, and usually hard-frozen until well into May; the other is Loch nan Stuirteag, between Braeriach and Monadh Mór. Even as recently as thirty years ago there were no seagulls nesting on these mountain lochs.

The black-headed gull has formed the new habit of flying up to the highest hills almost daily. It may be seen feeding on June evenings on the Braeriach plateau at 4,000 feet, beside the Wells of Dee, on the black mountain moths. These suck the nectar from the blossoms of the cushion pink, which beautify the Braeriach plateau at midsummer. In the years before the first war it was rare to see a black-headed gull here. Another bird which has moved up comparatively recently to nest on the Cairngorms is the lapwing, which in places nests actually in ptarmigan country.

There is a curious change in the numbers of that cunning stealer of eggs and young birds, the grey or hooded crow, known usually as the 'hoodie'. Fifty years ago, the grey crow was numerous in the forests of native Scots fir in Mar and Rothiemurchus. Its close relative, the carrion crow, was then almost unknown. My impression is that the carrion crow is now as numerous on Mar as the hooded crow.

The raven fifty years ago was unknown on Upper Deeside, but it now nests sparingly in Mar and elsewhere on Upper Deeside. On Deeside the buzzard was formerly unknown, but now nests over a wide area. This increase is the more remarkable since the rabbit, which is the buzzard's chief food, has been decimated and in some districts almost wiped out by myxomatosis. Like the buzzard, the wild cat has increased in this area, where fifty years ago it was on the verge of extinction.

While I am writing about Deeside, I must mention a remarkable change in the beautiful Moor of Dinnet in the last thirty years. Deeside-lovers will remember the glory of this moor when its bell heather was out in early July, and again when the ling was in bloom in August. At that time there was scarcely a birch tree on the moor. Despite every effort to check their spread, a forest of young birch has taken the place of the heather. No one knows what has brought about this sudden change. An explanation might lie in the absence of stock to graze down the young trees. But no sheep or cattle have been grazed here in living memory. This young birch forest has affected the bird life of the moor. Curlew, golden plover, and grouse are much fewer than in past decades.

In the Hebrides the most striking increase among the birds nesting on sea cliffs is in the fulmar, although these birds have not as yet established their habit of nesting inland—a habit which is firmly established in the Orkney and Shetland Islands. There has been a noticeable decrease in the number of lesser black-backed gulls in Skye. It is not generally known that the lesser black-back is a migrant and moves down to the coast of West Africa in winter. In March they return, and I used to see many pairs on the fields with the herring gulls in late March and throughout April, before they had begun to nest. Their numbers to be seen during recent years are noticeably fewer.

There is a decrease in the puffin and razorbill population of the Ascrib Islands in Loch Snisort and on the Fladday Chuain group since pre-war years, but a new kittiwake colony was founded about 1930 on Rudha Hunish, the northern promontory of Skye. I am afraid that during recent seasons almost all the young kittiwakes have been taken in the nest by that arch-robber, the greater black-headed gull.

I notice a considerable decrease in the numbers of barnacle geese, which used to winter on the fields in the north of Skye. Throughout one winter and early spring they frequented a grass field near our house and gave great pleasure. One morning when the geese were close to me I noticed that a barnacle goose had a Canada goose as mate, and I wondered whether, when the pair flighted north to Greenland (which is the nesting home of most of the barnacle geese wintering in the Hebrides), hybrid goslings might result from the unusual mating.

The effects of the great frost of the first two months of 1947 are still seen in Skye and elsewhere in Scotland. That frost wiped out the lapwing and stonechat population in Skye. I do not think that a single pair of stonechats nested in Skye that season, and of the many lapwings which formerly nested throughout the island I do not think that more than one pair survived. Both species have again increased, but not to anything like their former numbers.

On the Scottish mainland there was a similar decrease in the numbers of nesting curlew. In some districts, notably at Corrour in the Loch Treig country, they have never returned. But even before the great frost of 1947, the corn bunting was decreasing in its western haunts. This large bunting, too lazy to 'retract its under-carriage' when flying from one singing post to another, nests in hay or growing corn, and may have eggs as late as August. Its unmusical song, uttered usually as the bird surveys the scene from a telegraph wire, is heard in late summer, long after the lark is silent. My impression is that the corn bunting is now almost extinct in Skye, and everywhere in Scotland it is now much scarcer than it used to be.

We are in danger of losing the corncrake as a nesting species. It does not seem able to cope with modern methods of agriculture, despite the fact that its egg-clutch is an unusually large one. Its last nesting grounds will probably be in the Hebrides, but even here it is decreasing. The corncrake is a sedentary bird and rarely takes flight. It always seems to me little short of miraculous that at the end of the nesting season, with no preparation, it can take the air mysteriously and fly over land and across the sea, unseen, to Africa.

During the past half-century the blackbird has become bolder and more numerous in Scotland. Nowhere is this increase more noticeable than in the north lands of the Isle of Skye. By reason of its conspicuous plumage and melodious song the blackbird advertises itself and cannot well be missed, and I do not think there were more than two pairs of the species in northern Skye thirty years ago. Now there are few gardens or thickets without a pair or more, and the birds are becoming increasingly tame. In early November many hundreds of immigrant blackbirds arrive in Skye from Russia and the Baltic to reinforce, and battle with, the resident population.

There has been a change in the wild swan population of Scotland during the last fifty years. We have two species of wild swan, which are superficially alike although their nesting haunts lie many hundreds of miles apart. The lordly whooper is the larger of the two species. Its nesting places are mainly in Iceland. The smaller Bewick's swan (it receives its name from the north-country naturalist Bewick, who first recognized it as a distinct species) nests in distant Siberia and might therefore, one imagines, be perilously near the site of recent atomic explosions.

Fifty years ago Bewick's swan was more numerous in Scotland than the whooper swan. I used to watch a herd of at least 150 Bewick's swans swimming on Loch a' Phuill, on the Hebridean island of Tiree. Not a single Bewick's swan is to be seen now. Indeed, I know no loch throughout Scotland where this small swan can be found in any numbers. The whooper swan, on the other hand, has increased throughout the Scottish Highlands, and also in parts of the Lowlands, where Loch Leven shelters large numbers throughout the autumn and winter months. Some farmers blame the whooper swans for grazing their autumn-sown wheat.

Looking back on half a century, I see that interest in nature has greatly increased. Fifty years ago there were many people who liked to read about wild life, but did not have that enthusiasm in exploring for themselves which is so characteristic of the present generation. The love for hill-wandering was comparatively rare. It must be sixty years ago since I was approached by a weary party of tourists some miles to the west of the top of Lochnagar, while I was stalking and photographing a dotterel. It was a hot, sunny day. The only man in the party was wearing a broad white hat. When he removed it I saw that he had cabbage leaves on his head. As he wiped the sweat from his brow he said, 'This is a terrible place; are you not lonely here?'

I had begun to write articles when I was fourteen or fifteen years old. When I was seventeen a correspondent wrote that he was anxious to meet me. When he arrived I realized that he was at a loss to begin the conversation, for, as he said later, he had visualized me as an old gentleman with a white beard!

In the last fifty years I see a more tolerant attitude among many game preservers towards birds of prey which in the old days they would have classed as vermin. In the Highland deer forests there was always a friendly feeling for the eagle, but on grouse moors the eagle was soon quietly liquidated. A Highland proprietor told me that he would gladly leave the eagles on his land if he was given a subsidy for the number of grouse they caught.

But I am sure (although there are exceptions) a more tolerant attitude is now shown towards birds of prey, although the wild cat is still relentlessly pursued.

An unexpected bird, the collared dove, has recently colonized many parts of the Highlands. This year, 1970, we had twelve pairs in our plantation in the north of the Isle of Skye. The collared dove came from south-east Europe, arriving on the coast of Norfolk twenty-five years ago; the species has spread across Scotland and is in numbers on the Outer Hebrides, where it nests. If it continues on its north-west course it may reach Iceland nearly 800 miles away.

Close to the Golden Eagle

In 1958 the winter was not severe until March, but an exceptional blizzard, lasting for more than a fortnight, caught the golden eagle population just as the laying season arrived. It says much for this bird's stamina that two pairs, old acquaintances of mine, successfully weathered the storm.

For a fortnight the snow was knee- and sometimes thigh-deep, but on 16 March, a day of warm sunshine, I was able, by following the ridges, to reach a knoll from which one eyrie was visible. It was an Arctic scene and the March sun shone with power on the snowy expanse. The eagles' rock rose deep in snow; the male bird which often mounts guard on a neighbouring ridge was not to be seen, and no life was visible in the eyrie. It would, indeed, have been surprising if the birds had not deserted, but as I spied the eyrie, long and carefully, I saw a dark shape rise a few inches, then gradually subside. A little later I saw this movement again—it was the brooding eagle's back, as it moved on the nest. When I returned to the road a snow-plough was battering at the great wreaths which the previous day's gale had piled above older and harder drifts.

On 17 March a frozen crust on the snow permitted me to make easier progress to another eyrie. It is perhaps to assert their territorial claim that golden eagles sometimes repair the eyrie before the end of the year. Unlike most pairs, this had only one nest and it had been repaired before Christmas. I had not visited the pair for some time and when I saw the overhanging snow cornice and the depth of snow on the ledges I was doubtful whether they had been able to keep their eyrie free of snow during the egg-laying period, which is usually from 8 March to 15 March.

I had watched the rock while the sun crept round towards the west, and had almost decided to leave when the male bird sailed in and alighted on a sun-bathed ridge sheltered from the wind. Here it preened carefully, dozed, and yawned hugely. Near by a pair of half-starved lapwings searched listlessly for food where the sun had melted the snow, and a pair of ravens in strong flight crossed high overhead.

This eyrie leads into a recess, and so the brooding eagle is seldom visible, but I inferred from the presence of the male that she was brooding. I was on the point of leaving when the male took wing, sailed backwards and forwards along the face of the cliff several times, and then made a landing at the eyrie, now a large, imposing structure. It walked into the recess, anxious, I think, to change over, but the female would not oblige, although I saw her move. The male then stood on the rim of the eyrie as if in thought, looked about, and several times picked up in its strong bill pieces of heather which lay near the nest, building them deftly into the eyrie.

Now followed a most interesting incident. About three feet below, the bird saw a particularly attractive branch. As it peered over, it lost its balance and half-fell to where the heather lay, steadying itself with its wings as it dropped. It picked up the heather, and I watched to see whether it would climb, with difficulty perhaps, up to the eyrie, or would travel by air. It made a quick decision. Throwing itself with a grand gesture over the cliff it sailed for a short distance, and then, reaching an ascending thermal, rose buoyantly, sailed back along the cliff at the correct elevation and made a skilled landing on the eyrie with the heather branch.

For nearly a month winter lingered in the golden eagles' country. Then, on the last day of March, without warning, came the first day of spring. That afternoon, as my wife and I watched the eyrie beneath courting lapwings, the sun shone brilliantly on the long snow-cornice which curled over into space above the eagles' rock, Here, beneath the cliff, was wheatear ground, yet it seemed beyond possibility that any of these birds would have come all the way from their winter quarters on the roof of Kenya to arrive at a time when the snow was still on the ground in Skye.

Below us, indistinct bird calls were heard, and then the unexpected happened—on a moss-covered boulder a cock wheatear in its handsome nesting dress stood, very much at home, preening the delicately coloured plumage of neck and back. It is usually the rule that the male wheatears arrive at the nesting ground before the hens, so it was even more surprising to see near it a hen bird, presumably its mate. Harsh calls from a pair of grey crows on rocky ground across the corrie increased in volume as the two birds appeared in pursuit of the female golden eagle, a very large bird with an unusually light-coloured plumage. This was the eagle which I had seen the previous summer stoop at and miss a rabbit, and then run like a dog to the entrance of the rabbit's burrow, and peer eagerly into it. This was also the bird which had dive-bombed its eaglet time after time as the young bird was standing after its first flight on the cliff top. Finally it had taken a rabbit to its bewildered and chastened offspring.

Ignoring the attention of the crows the eagle suddenly increased speed, and we saw that it was seeing a greater black-backed gull off its territory. It then sailed in to the cliff, alighted beyond our view and, as it reappeared a little later, we saw that it carried a long, slender branch in its bill. The gusty wind caught the bird as it sailed in spirals close to the rock before alighting at the eyrie where, as I have recorded, exactly a fortnight before its mate had been filling in its time by doing small repairs to the nest. Now, I thought to myself, we shall see the change-over. As the female stood in bright sunshine, at the edge of the eyrie, its plumage seemed almost white.

Minutes passed and nothing happened. Then at last, from a recess beyond our view, the mate rose slowly and even reluctantly from the eggs. As it walked to the edge of the eyrie the relative darkness of its plumage was striking. This was normal golden eagle plumage; that of its mate was exceptional. The two eagles stood side by side, facing opposite directions, then the female walked slowly into the recess to the eggs and the male dropped into the abyss, spread wide its broad wings and passed directly over our heads as it set out on an expedition for food.

Thus, within ten brief minutes, we had our first view of a pair of wheatears and had seen an exciting change-over at the eyrie of the eagles.

Golden Eagles Mating

The March blizzard had deeply covered the hills, and the eagles' rock rose grim and lonely beneath a sombre sky. High on this snowy rock were the two eyries which the eagles have used, regularly in alternate seasons, during the past twenty years. Now, when the eagles should have been busy at their house repairs, the eyries were buried and unrecognizable beneath the snow which lay on each ledge of that high cliff.

I have watched the home life of these eagles during each of the twenty seasons they have nested here and have come to know how near the observer can approach and sit without alarming the birds. It was cold on the sunless, snowy slope and I was about to end my watch, for there had been no sign of the eagles, nor of the pair of ravens which share, rather unwillingly, the eagles' territory. The eagle-watcher often experiences an unexpected thrill at the moment he is preparing to leave his station, and it was fortunate for me that I was reluctant to start for home.

The two golden eagles appeared, coming suddenly into my view from the far side of the cliff. The male was leading. He is, as is well known, smaller than his mate, but I have also come to recognize him by his poise, and by his buoyant and almost delicate soaring. He is, besides, unusually attentive and when the eggs were near hatching I have watched him almost push his mate off the eyrie in order to take his share in incubating the eggs during this critical period. Now, within a week of when the eggs should be laid, the two eagles seemed to be taking life easily, with no thought of rearing a family.

Pesticides used in sheep dip are thought to be changing the golden eagle's pattern of life and, indeed, so far as I could tell, this pair of eagles reared no young during the season of 1964. Was the coming season to be a barren one also? The female eagle rose buoyantly, for she felt the uprising current beneath a passing snow cloud. From a height of several hundred feet she glided gracefully down and alighted on a rocky spur above the precipice. In less than a minute her mate alighted close to her. They stood there in proud and majestic beauty—the King and Queen of Birds!

19

Her mate walked up to her, jumped lightly on to her back and mating took place. His six-foot wings were outspread and half-raised. This mating lasted perhaps a couple of minutes, when the male eagle sprang lightly into the air and disappeared from my view. Then came a most impressive joy flight by his mate. Rising to a great height on an air current she closed her wings and pressed them tightly against her flanks, going into an almost vertical dive. When near the ledge where one of the eyries is situated she suddenly straightened out, again sailed to her former height, and again performed that exciting headlong descent.

This was the 'display' which both male and female golden eagle at times perform. There is nothing more impressive in the bird world than to see a pair of eagles, sometimes together, carry out, in obvious enjoyment, a series of tremendous dives followed by rapid climbs.

On this March afternoon the female, after her aerobatics, had scarcely alighted on her rocky perch when a pair of ravens, her neighbours on the same heathery cliff, passed over at a great height. Travelling fast, one of the ravens with a sudden movement turned on its back and for a second flew 'upside-down' in unique raven fashion. The sight of the eagle far below it may have prompted this display.

The previous afternoon I had watched the eagles hunting. A fresh north-easter was blowing across the cliff, and the eagles were hunting it carefully for their main food, the rabbit. They would glide at great speed downwind across the snowy slope, then slowly move up against the wind, dark objects casting still darker shadows on the white, snow-filled gullies. Small avalanches were falling from a snow-cornice along the hill top and the eagles dropped suddenly to the falling fragments of snow and carefully inspected them; they may have thought that a rabbit was in the snow. Near sunset one of the eagles during the patrol up-wind made a sudden, rapid slant to lower ground.

His keen eye had detected a rabbit, which he killed instantly and carefully plucked the fur from the carcass before enjoying his supper. He then lifted the remains and, as he slowly rose in spirals, looked like a miniature airship. Having gained sufficient height he sailed in and alighted on a ledge near the eyrie, where he was joined by his mate and perhaps shared his supper with her.

Now to add a footnote, on the evening after this chapter was written. In sunshine this afternoon I arrived at my observation post less than a minute before the eagles together alighted on the eyrie which they had built last year but had not nested in it. This eyrie, which two days previously had been buried in snow, was now almost snow-free, and this was evidently a house inspection. After two inspections the male sailed out of sight and the female slanted in a different direction. In three minutes she fought her way back against the strong breeze along the ridges, carrying a tuft of dead grass in her bill.

She alighted and laid it carefully on the nest. The repairs to the home had begun! Three times in less than half an hour after sailing at impressive speed down-wind for perhaps a mile she returned with building material; the two tufts of grass were carried in the bill and a heather root in one foot. I watched her, with wildly flapping wings, endeavour to uproot a heather plant, but it held firm despite her strength.

After this effort she sunbathed for some time on a sheltered spur. Her quick eyes detecting a movement far below, she launched out, sped low over ground, still snow-covered, and suddenly checked her flight. The rabbit may have gone to earth, for the eagle, still gliding low, next put up a flock of migrating lapwings but seemed uninterested in them—no doubt a rabbit was a more satisfying meal than a green plover. Quickly climbing to a height of some 2,000 feet, she was joined by her mate and they vanished from my view, steering towards a distant rabbit-haunted corrie.

Skye Keeps its Norwegian Accent

In the Norse sagas, one of the first references to Skye was its subjection in the year 1098 by King Magnus of Norway: in the sagas its name is given as Skith. The form Skye is first found in 1498. A century and a half after King Magnus subdued the island, Skye was an isle of Norway rather than of Scotland.

This was the position when the Earl of Ross made a bitter attack on Skye in 1262. In the summer of that year an urgent letter was brought to King Haco of Norway from the Norse Jarl who ruled the Isle of Skye, informing the king of the Scottish invasion. The invaders, in the words of the Saga, 'had let small bairns sprawl on their spear-points and cast them dead off them.'

In August of the next year, 1263, King Haco sailed with his war galleys for Scotland. He sailed south past Cape Wrath (itself a Norse word) and then through the strait that has ever since been known as Caol Akin, Haco's Strait. The name is now given to the village of Kyleakin, which stands on the Skye shore opposite Kyle of Lochalsh on the mainland.

In the year 1266 Norway ceded the Isle of Skye and the rest of the Hebrides to Scotland, but it was stipulated that a certain sum was to be paid yearly by Scotland to Norway as tribute money. It might be interesting to bring the terms of this historic agreement to the notice of King Olav and to ascertain whether his Government is still receiving an annual payment.

It is remarkable that, seven centuries exactly after Norse rule had ended in Skye, fully half of the more important place-names on the island remain Norse. The seven natural provinces of the isle have Norse names. They are: Trotternish, Vaternish, Duirinish, Minginish, Bracadale, Strathordil, and Sleat.

The Celtic scholar MacBain believes that Trotternish is another form of the Icelandic Thondarnes, and means Thrond's Ness, Thrond being a favourite Norwegian personal name. Vaternish, he says, finds its counterpart in the Icelandic Vatnsnes, Water Ness; Ness or Nose being the Norse word used to denote Cape. Arnish, Cape of the Erne or Sea Eagle, commemorates the Sea or White-tailed Eagle, now extinct as a nesting species in Scotland, but still found on the Lofoten Islands in Norway.

Many of the Skye hills have Norwegian names, but at a later date the Celts added the Gaelic word 'Beinn,' a hill, to the Norse original. This is well seen in the present-day name for the attractive hill guarding Portree Bay to the south. It is Beinn Tianavaig. The original Norse name was Tindar Vik, Peak Bay, from the proximity of the hill. The word Vik, in its Gaelic form Uig, is still found on the north wing of Skye.

Another example of a hybrid place-name is found in Beinn Storr, an imposing hill about six miles north-east of Portree. The late Professor W. J. Watson had no doubt that the original name was given to the great pillar of rock, now known as The Old Man of Storr. The word Storr meant Stake, and there was no 'Beinn' in the original name. Perhaps centuries later, when the Norse influence had waned, the people of Skye added the word Beinn, and now the name is Beinn Storr.

During his visit to Dunvegan Castle King Olav of Norway could see, across the loch, Husabost and Boreraig. The Norse word Bost, meaning a township, occurs in many Hebridean place-names. Husabost is now the home of one of the Martins of Skye, men distinguished by their tremendous strength and their courage in grappling with the ferocious, supernatural Each Uisge or Water Horse.

Beyond Husabost is Boreraig, which again shows the Norse termination vik. Here was the home of the immortal MacCrimmon pipers; had they still been there it is certain that they would have composed a 'Failte' or Salute to His Majesty King Olav. The ruins of the MacCrimmon College of Piping are here, and the College of Piping in Glasgow have hopes of rebuilding this historic landmark and teaching pupils the tunes which were composed by the Mac-Crimmons and have been handed down through the generations.

A pupil at the MacCrimmon College was instructed only in Ceòl Mór, the Great Music or Piobaireachd. Before he could win the coveted MacCrimmon Diploma he was required to memorize and play without fault 199 compositions in Ceòl Mór.

No MacCrimmon Diploma survives, as far as is known. There is said to have been one, half a century ago, in the possession of a family of the name of Robertson in Inverness. It is said that a picture of Dunvegan Castle and of MacLeod's Galley were on it, and also various musical instruments. The MacCrimmon seal completed this work of art. Sir Walter Scott tells us a little of MacCrimmon piping during his visit to Dunvegan Castle a century and a half ago.

When King Olav flew by helicopter across the Minch to Benbecula at the close of his visit to Dunvegan he could see Hunish, the most northerly cape of Skye. This Norse place-name is from the old Norse word Hunn, a Bear, and is generally believed to be a personal name here. There may be another explanation. It is not generally known that guarding Hunish is a great boulder which has an extraordinarily vivid resemblance to a bear sitting on its haunches. The ears, nose, eyes, and even the expression of the bear are seen, and I have often thought that this is the true explanation of the place-name.

On the Moors of Upper Deeside

The upper reaches of the Dee Valley in Aberdeenshire are celebrated for their moors. Near the end of July of a recent year a visit to that part of the Highlands (the Burn of Dinnet is said to have been the dividing line between the Highlands and Lowlands) showed me that the bloom on the heather was likely to be exceptional. By 'heather', I mean the ling (*Calluna vulgaris*) whose flowering season is August; but before the end of July the bell heather (*Erica cinerea*) was clothing dry hill slopes in purple, and in one place I had the unusual experience of seeing the less common cat heather (*Erica tetralix*) covering a large area of ground with delicate pink.

What is the secret of a good heather year? Old stalkers and keepers believed that there was a short period on the threshold of summer when the weather was all-important for the heather crop. That year the last week in May gave some of the warmest days experienced in the Highlands and gave the plants a good start. It might have been thought that the Arctic spell that followed might have nipped the young shoots. The severity of that spell may be judged from the fact that on June 19th the highest temperature at the newly established weather station on the shoulder of Cairngorm, at a height of 3,650 feet, was only one degree above freezing point, and the snow-fall over a large area of high ground did not entirely melt for a fortnight.

July was mild, although the browned shoots of young spruce and the red fronds of the hated bracken remained as memorials of the June frosts. Nowhere did the heather or ling promise a better flowering season than in Glen Callater, south of Braemar. Loch Callater, 1,627 feet above sea level, is reached in early July by salmon after a long journey from the North Sea by way of the Dee and the Cluny. This may, indeed, be the highest loch in the Scottish Highlands to contain salmon; the fish, already dark in colour, were throwing themselves with abandon out of the peaty water.

It is in Glen Callater that the old drovers' track known as Jock's Road crosses the hills to Angus. This track is not easy to follow when snow lies on the ground; early in January some years ago a number of climbers lost their lives there in a sudden blizzard. As one walks

C

south along Jock's Road a spectacular waterfall drops in a series of white cascades from the high ground and holds the eye. Here is the haunt of the ring ousel.

The flowers of the yellow saxifrage grow in the spray, and a wandering kestrel was sailing high above Coire Ceanndor on the dark and still afternoon when a friend and I climbed to the lonely shore of Loch Ceanndor. This clear hill loch is well named 'Loch at the Head of the High Water'. The name in Gaelic is written Loch Ceann Dobhar; the word *dobhar* is used in old Gaelic for a hill stream that flows swiftly down from the high ground. Loch Ceanndor lies at the heart of a rocky corrie, Coire Ceanndor. My friend and I admired the easy manner in which the lone kestrel patrolled this great corrie, covering in less than two minutes an area of steep ground a climber would take a day to traverse. Each time it passed the kestrel lingered above a grassy strip; perhaps a mouse had caught the bird's attention on a previous foray.

We were scarcely as high as ptarmigan ground, but on our return journey, when we left the path and crossed the heathery slopes, we soon realized that red grouse here had done well that year in their nesting. Coveys were numerous, and the young birds were already fully grown, although there was still a fortnight and more until the morning of the twelfth.

Although there had been a snowstorm of considerable severity in June, the winter had been mild, and on the clear morning two days later when we travelled west up the Dee valley from Invercauld, the Laird's Tablecloth on Beinn a' Bhuird (3,900 feet) had already disappeared from sight. This is a great snowfield that sometimes remains unmelted throughout the summer and autumn. It is said that the Farquharsons of Invercauld held their land on condition that they were able to give the King of Scotland a bucket of snow at any time he should demand it. In a warm summer, when the Tablecloth melted, the Laird of Invercauld was accustomed to say that the snow was so discoloured that it was invisible from the valley below. A number of Highland families are traditionally said to have held their land under what might be termed 'snow tenure'. Names that occur to me are the Munros of Foulis, the Camerons of Lochiel and the Grants of Rothiemurchus.

The high hills attract many climbers. Despite pesticides and climbing parties, the golden eagle still nests on its ancestral lands in the Dee valley. Not all climbers are bird-minded. A stalker told us an amusing story. Earlier that summer a climber hurried up to him and said: 'Keeper, I saw the biggest crow of my life perched on top of a fir tree up the glen. Get your gun and shoot it.' From the description given him, the stalker knew that the 'biggest crow' was none other than an eagle. He pacified the climber, thanked him for his valuable information, and saw him set out towards the distant village whence he had come.

Near the headwaters of the Dee, one is at the heart of the High Cairngorms. In the sixty summers I have known them the old Scots firs have changed little, but their numbers are fewer. In Preas nam Meirleach, the Robbers' Thicket, where the cattle raiders from Lochaber used to hide, there is now little room for concealment. From the highest ground of the track as it crosses the shoulder of Carn a' Mhaim we could hear the croaking of invisible ptarmigan on the Devil's Point across the valley more than a mile away, and could see diaphanous mist dissolving on the upper slopes of Cairntoul. To the west was Glen Giusachan, one of the most lonely glens of the Cairngorms, where fir trees that lived one thousand years and more ago are sometimes exposed by the river in times of spate.

An unexpected sight appeared as we 'spied' Glen Giusachan. A great herd of Hereford cattle were slowly making their way in single file up the glen. They must have strayed from a neighbouring glen where they usually are pastured, and were evidently finding their new home to their liking. We wondered when cattle in such numbers had last been seen in Glen Giusachan. In far-distant days Highland raiders must have passed this way with the cattle they had 'lifted' from the fertile lands of the east, but the beasts on those occasions would have been driven relentlessly by armed men. Those we now saw were obviously happy and undisturbed as they made their way up a glen unknown to them, rich in pasture and sheltered from the wind.

It was strange indeed to see cattle in such numbers where no living man had seen them before; almost as strange was it to search in vain with the telescope for the great snow-bed on the face of Monadh Mór, the high hill that guards the glen to the west. It is often September before it melts, and it is not unusual to find it undefeated until it is reinforced by the new snow of the following winter. Rare indeed is it to see Monadh Mór without snow at the end of July before the flowering of the ling.

The Song of the Curlew

In late April and throughout May the song of the curlew is heard at its best. Nightingale and skylark have inspired poets but the curlew has never been thus immortalized. Lord Grey of Fallodon, a poet at heart, has I think, written the best descriptions of its song, for he said in his *Charm of Birds* that there is in that song of beauty the blend of happiness, thankfulness and sadness.

Those of us who love the song of the curlew treasure the experience of hearing it from one year to the next and if our home is outside the spring and summer area of the singer we cheerfully travel miles to hear it. My own memories of the song are linked with Ardura and Glen Mor in the Isle of Mull, and with the hill country of Northumberland between Catcleugh and Carter Bar. In Mull the curlews waken the sleeping hills in late March where a small moss-grown cairn marks the death of a chieftain centuries ago. In late April the song grows stronger and more confident and it continues throughout May. Indeed, I remember exceptional singing of curlews here as late as the second week in June, music which was the more appreciated because one realized that it would soon be at an end. On the moors of Northumberland I first discovered that the hen curlew is as accomplished a singer as her mate. Here one has, or had, the special and memorable pleasure of listening to perhaps half a dozen pairs of curlews singing at the same time.

The song flight of the curlew begins with a tremulous beating of the wings, then a short glide during which a single low musical whistle is uttered. This tremulous rising and gentle descent, with the accompaniment of a single deep musical whistle, may be repeated a dozen times or more as the curlew flies low above the moor. It is but a prelude, and sometimes the curlew never gets beyond this 'tuning up'. The song proper begins with the single low note of the prelude and then the listener hears a series of clear, urgent whistles in a rising key, the music gradually becoming faster and more impetuous. The song may be sustained at its highest pitch for perhaps a quarter of a minute when the music slows down and, in a descending key, ends in a long, sorrowful note. Occasionally the curlew sings on the ground, but then the song is hardly ever so long or so thrilling in quality. The bird loves a calm mild day for its singing, and soft rain encourages the singer.

Moorlands and rough pastures are its spring and summer home, but it does not rest so high on the hills as does the golden plover. It is a rare nester on the Isle of Skye, and I have never heard of or seen a nest in the Outer Hebrides. Its range on the mainland has increased and it now nests on water meadows between Oxford and Banbury, but at its chief haunts it is nowhere so numerous as it was in the years immediately before the first world war. A piece of bagpipe music called 'The Curlew' was recently composed by Donald MacPherson, one of the leading pipers of the present day.

A Rare Highland Flower

On a Highland hilltop (it must remain nameless) is the only known colony in Britain of that rare plant of the high north, *Diapensia lapponica*: it is a tribute to its rarity that it has, so far as I am aware, no Scottish or English name. This relic of a colder climate and era was discovered by accident, by an ornithologist.

Like most Alpine and Arctic plants, it is of recumbent habit. Its small leaves are close-pressed to the ground, but its reddish-brown flower stems may rise several inches from the parent cushion. The flowers are comparatively large. They are white, sometimes with a yellowish tinge. The corolla, with the stamens, is easily shed: a strong wind is sufficient to scatter the flower-heads, the petals still attached at the base, upon the lichen-covered ground at the lee of the colony.

The homeland of *Diapensia lapponica*, as may be inferred from its scientific name, is Lapland. It is remarkable that the Scottish colony, which may be a relic of an earlier flora of a different climate, should have remained undiscovered until recently.

A drought of more than three weeks in the Scottish Highlands was nearing its close when a companion and I set out to climb to the remote hilltop which is the home of *Diapensia*, exposed to gales and storms even in summer. The burn flowing through the glen was at its lowest ebb, but light rain had fallen early that morning, checking a moorland fire which the previous day had filled the air with smoke.

At a height of 1,500 feet above the sea the clear water flowed through a gorge. Here a small colony of globe flowers were seen. One of the golden flowers was of quite exceptional size. There was no wind, the air was heavy, and mist hid the high hills ahead of us. In the glen the butterwort had opened its dark blue flowers, but at 2,000 feet scarcely a flower bud was showing. The red flowers of the lousewort, sometimes in small colonies, gave a touch of colour to the sombre ground.

At 2,500 feet a northerly air, cold and vital, flowed from the mist cap; it might well have had its origin above some distant icefield or snowy mountain. Grey clouds slowly ebbed and flowed; from behind the ridge there came, unexpectedly, a lightning flash. The distant call of a cuckoo came faintly on that air from a gully, perhaps a mile distant, where rowan and birch grew almost from the solid rock; near us a raven circled, croaking.

A small flowering cushion of the creeping azalea showed us that we had approached the country of *Diapensia*, but the ridge was broad and it was not easy to locate the colony. Not only is *Diapensia lapponica* rare but it is a plant of charm and character. Its flowers are distinctive, but at a little distance one might imagine for a moment that one was approaching a colony of *Dryas octopetala* in flower.

In an average season *Diapensia* is in flower early in June. On this dark morning of early summer there were many open flowers, many buds, and one or two flowers that were already going to seed. The colony did not look happy. The long dry spell, followed by days of strong, cold, north winds, which brought snow and hail to the high tops, had caught the plants as they were beginning to flower.

As I have mentioned earlier in this essay, the flowers, each on a single stem, are normally white, with a slight yellow tinge. This year the yellow is more pronounced, and the flower stems are shorter than usual. In a mountain plant, growing under severe conditions, it is curious that corolla and stamens are sometimes shed even at the touch of a human hand. One or two plants of the colony, in slight shelter from the rock, were in better shape and no doubt a spell of warmer and damper weather would alter the appearance of the colony.

We came upon a lochan entirely dry, and saw in its peaty bed the tracks of a red deer. The light strengthened and a pale sun showed through the mist. Near us an unseen cock ptarmigan snorted and a wheatear alighted on a rock.

Amid the scattered rocks at a little distance from us a small torch seemed magically to be lighted. It glittered among the stones as though it marked the secret entrance to a fairy chamber beneath the ground. An investigation showed that this was mica, reflecting the sun's light: as the sun strengthened it shone more brightly, and was dim when a misty veil passed across the sun's face.

By mid-afternoon the clouds had lifted from the hills, but a thick haze remained. In the glen that evening the midges were active and the scent of rowan blossom and young birch leaves lay on the still air. One night of frost the previous week had caught the young bracken fronds and blackened them. On a journey of many miles by car through the Highlands we saw the effects of this frost, and there was accordingly little wonder that the hilltop colony of *Diapensia* should have suffered.

Handa's Monarchs of the Air

The high island of Handa rises from the Atlantic near Scourie, on the north coast of Sutherland. It was long ago named by the Norsemen Sanda or Handa, the Sand Island, because of the sandy beaches on its sheltered shores facing the mainland. The sea cliffs which form its west and north-west boundary are of red sandstone, and fall sheer 400 feet to the Atlantic. Until the year 1845 eight families lived here, but since then the island has been uninhabited, and is now a nature reserve.

Like the St Kildans, the people of Handa had their Queen. They also had their Parliament, which met each morning to discuss plans for the day. Handa was famed for the quality of its potatoes, manured with seaweed and grown in the warm, sandy soil. The isle in 1845 was abandoned because of the failure of this crop. The inhabitants lived mainly on potatoes, and when the crop failed because of blight the people, together with those on the near mainland, emigrated. The number leaving for Canada then was so great that five sailing ships had to be chartered for their voyage across the Atlantic.

The sea-bird colonies on Handa have long been celebrated. In the year 1901 there was excitement among ornithologists when the first fulmar's egg was found here. During recent years the great skua has also nested here successfully. It was late in August when my wife and I crossed the sea strait from Tarbet to the island. The day was sunny, clear and almost cloudless. On the south horizon the great rock pillar known as the Old Man of Storr was lifted in a mirage until its base seemed to rise almost clear of the sea. We steered across the passage known as Dorus Mór, the Great Door. Heavy seas flow through this strong tidal stream when the north-west wind blows, and Handa may be inaccessible for days at a time. There is, by the way, another Dorus Mór, more widely known by yachtsmen, between the mainland of Argyll and the Island of Jura. As we approached Handa on this tidal stream shags shot up like corks from their dives close to the boat, and on seeing us, instantly dived again. We landed on a beach of pinkish sand on which small, friendly waves broke. The sun was warm, the air fresh and vital as we climbed across the sand dunes and saw, nearly two miles ahead of us, the small cairn on the highest ground, our destination. The path to the cliffs, marked by a line of white-topped posts, winds near the ruins of houses and the old burial ground which is on the machair. Here are nameless graves, but on one recumbent stone larger than the rest the name PETER MORRISON can be read, but there is no date. The houses of Handa were well built and after more than a century the walls still stand.

The walker who approaches the sea cliffs of Handa from the eastern landing place has no hint that the gentle grassy slope is to end in a sheer precipice until he sees a fulmar, then another and another, flying ahead. Suddenly the edge of the cliff is reached and the high cliffs and the Atlantic beyond them are seen. Here are fulmars, gliding and soaring, swerving and wheeling, through their dominion. On the cliffs of Handa the bird lover might hope to find that very rare British bird, the sea eagle. It is just over a century ago (the date was 1864) that Handa lost its pair of sea eagles.

Harvie-Brown in his book *Fauna of the North West Highlands* puts it on record that in the year 1865 Donald Matheson, piper to the Duke of Westminster, pointed out to him the site of the sea eagles' eyrie on Handa. This was forty years before fulmars nested for the first time on Handa. Now there is a large breeding colony of fulmars here; the young are long in the nest, and do not fly until the beginning of September. On this day of late summer the fulmars, feathered but with whiter plumage than their parents, were performing vigorous wing exercises. They were careful to face the land during this wing-flapping so that they should not fly themselves out of the nesting hollow by mistake. Beyond the cliff lay the Atlantic, apparently calm at first sight. That tranquillity was deceptive. As we sat on a carpet of sea thrift, closely grazed by sheep, the air was permeated by the thunder of the swell as it entered invisible caverns beneath us or flung itself high against the rock walls. The deep voice of the ocean was impressive and the thunder of the waves 400 feet below us never ceased. For a few seconds the volume of sound lessened, but rose again to a deep muffled roar, long sustained.

Near the highest area on Handa is a lochan which might well be given the name Kittiwake Lochan. On any calm day in late May a white cloud of kittiwakes hover above this lochan as a continuous stream of these birds fly up from nesting ledges far down the cliff. These arrivals alight with obvious pleasure on the lochan to bathe. Their joyful bath ended, they rise on white black-tipped wings, shake the water from their plumage, and alight on the shore of the lochan. They stand there in orderly rows, but there is no time for rest or enjoyment. Each bird now eagerly pulls up grass and moss with its bill. When it can hold no more, it flies to the edge of the cliff and drops out of sight like a falling stone to its half-completed nest far below. Their early summer activities forgotten, the kitti-wakes at the time of our visit had gone to sea for the winter, and the air, this quiet sun-drenched afternoon, was vibrant with the excited guttural cries of fulmars, quickly repeated. The growling of invisible waves was a soothing accompaniment to these cries.

The mainland seemed far removed from this scene. Yet as I turned and looked east to the long barren ridge of Foinne Bheinn—a noble hill just short of 3,000 feet in height in the Reay Forest—I remembered the hot summer day many years ago when Dara the collie and I set out from Lochmore Lodge to cross the long ridge of Foinne Bheinn, on our walk to Gualan on the high ground above the Dionard River. At one place, near the cairn on the hill top, the sudden drop on the ridge is so steep, and the boulders so unstable, that Dara could scarcely be persuaded to follow me. The absence of any spring or burn was a trial on that twelve-hour walk and I remember our delight, late in the evening, when we found a spring of ice-cold water. Ben Stack, a neighbour of Foinne Bheinn, is an attractive cone-shaped hill several hundred feet lower. On one memorable occasion, from the cairn on Ben Stack I was able to see the distant Atlantic island of North Rona, on which the distinguished scientist Dr Frank Fraser Darling and his wife once spent a spartan winter while the whole island trembled with the force of the gigantic Atlantic waves.

On Handa that evening of late summer we watched the setting sun bathe Foinne Bheinn in golden light and as we left the soaring fulmars and walked east across the island to the landing place it was unexpected to see a sparrow hawk, a bird associated with wood-lands, fly past close to us on migration. That evening the sound of the Highland bagpipe, played by a piper at the edge of the tide on smooth untrodden sand as a signal to the ferryman a mile across the strait, alarmed inquisitive seals, and the white oystercatcher which lived on Handa for twenty years. As we travelled towards Ben Stack across the moors the fragrance of bog-myrtle and heather increased on the windless air, as twilight settled over land, sea and many lochs and lochans.

On a subsequent visit to Handa in mid-July the great bird colony was in residence but preparing to leave. Guillemots standing in lines on their whitened ledges as though on parade greet an approaching boat with a tremendous outcry that once heard will never be forgotten. Preparations for their departure to the Atlantic to spend the rest of the year there are made with much excitement and agitation. Our small undecked lobster boat left Tarbet on a day of sunshine. There was a strong breeze from the east, and as we cleared the shelter of the shore we saw the waves break dazzling white on the outer skerries. Terns plunged into the green water and shags fished, but as yet there was no hint of the nearness of a great seabird colony. We reached and crossed the tidal river and almost at once felt the power of the Atlantic swell. Our boat rose like a cork on the great walls of water eagerly approaching the high cliffs, their backwash causing a confused sea. We passed the ledge where sea eagles once nested, and were told of an immature bird of the species, perhaps one of the young birds brought from Norway the previous summer and reared on Fair Isle, which had been seen chasing fulmars that February.

Soon we found ourselves escorted by guillemots. The rock ledges on the sheer red sandstone cliff were crowded with these attractive, excitable birds. The guillemot lays only one egg, but it is large, pyriform, and beautifully streaked and marked with reddish-brown spots and blotches. No nest is made. The egg lies on the bare rock and the owner holds it on her foot while brooding. The chick is fed on sand-eels and small fry. Only one small fish is brought at a time, although the guillemot may have flown from fishing grounds fifty miles or more out to sea. It is strange that if a fish is dropped by accident on a ledge it is never picked up, either by parent or chick; another long journey to the fishing grounds is then undertaken. When it leaves the ledge the young bird is still in down. It is understandably reluctant to throw itself from a height into the boiling sea and is therefore called repeatedly and encouragingly by its parent swimming below the cliff. Gradually it summons up courage and, its stumpy wings whirring, risks the fateful drop. It is sometimes killed by a projecting ledge, but usually reaches the water safely. Here even more grim dangers confront it before it can reach the open ocean. Eagerly awaiting it are sinister great black-backed gulls, bird tyrants of the first order. As the mother (only one parent is usually present on these occasions) swims with the baby away from the base of the cliff, one or more of these gulls swoops down and attempts to carry off the small swimmer. Even at this early stage the young guillemot is able to dive, but it cannot remain submerged for long. When it comes to the surface the gull is ready to pounce and time after time the guillemot is forced under until it is exhausted, and eaten by the enemy.

Below the sea cliff of Handa, at its greatest height, a low shelf of rock projects seaward, at low tide just above the water's surface. Here confused seas were breaking high and as we neared this formidable hazard I wondered idly what would happen if our outboard engine failed. At this very minute the engine slowed down and then stopped: it remained silent despite repeated efforts by our boatman to coax it into life. Wind and tide were now bearing us unpleasantly near this ledge, against which waves were leaping to a height of at least fifteen feet. A landing here would have been impossible, for the cliff is sheer. Oars were in the boat, and by rowing seawards against wind and breaking seas we were able to reach a tidal river which carried us past the reef.

It was now as we drifted with the tide that, as bird lovers, we watched a remarkable sight. Scores of guillemots were swimming on the sea near us. While our engine was functioning the birds kept at a respectful distance, but now, as we drifted silently, they swam near, looking at us intently. Soon they began to dive under the boat, playfully, as it seemed. The sun shone into the green ocean depths and the guillemots, perhaps twelve feet below the surface, could be seen clearly as they passed beneath the boat. They moved fast, using their wings as oars; it was interesting to note that the birds as they swam rolled first on one side, then on the other. During these rolls the white breast and under parts flashed snow-white deep down in the water. This exhibition was the highlight of our expedition round Handa. It is possible that the birds imagined we were fishing and that small fry might be attracted by our bait. The engine now came to life and in less than five minutes we had passed beyond the turbulent seas and high cliffs to the pink-tinged sands which nearly a thousand years ago gave Handa its name.

Recently a large piratical bird, the great skua or bonxie, has made its summer home on Handa and several pairs nest on the island. The great skua is a pirate and as I was once sailing round the high island of Noss in Shetland I saw one of these birds perform a feat which must be very rare. Solans or gannets have a nesting colony on Noss, and great skuas await, over the sea, to intercept any gannet returning with fish for its young. They harry the victim until it disgorges the fish, when the skua dives after it and catches it before it reaches the water. A gannet flying high over the boat was attacked but continued its flight with determination until the great skua alighted on its back and with wings outspread to maintain its precarious balance, hammered the back of the victim's neck with its powerful bill as it continued to fly, until the fish was disgorged, when it was deftly caught in mid-air. This was perhaps the most exciting incident I have seen in a long life of bird watching. The Handa great skuas may be better behaved, but I heard of a visitor who approached a nest hatless and was struck on the head with such violence by the angry bird that blood flowed as he hurried back to the boat.

Swallows on Migration

One is not often fortunate enough to witness the arrival and passage of a large flight of swallows on migration. Last spring I was at my wife's home, Biddlesden Park, near Brackley, Northamptonshire. Below the house, which was formerly an abbey, and where the fourteenth-century barn is still in use, is a long narrow lake, surrounded by old deciduous trees. The trees were still leafless, but a moist and mild south wind had aroused many insects from their winter torpor, and now they were being blown off the trees and grass into a pocket of quiet air beside a stream. Many swallows had arrived on passage and, despite heavy rain, were hawking insects there. It was strange to see the swallows, their hunger satisfied for the time being, alight on the topmost branches of the swaying trees forty or fifty feet above the ground. There perched close together in pairs like budgerigars they twittered happily one to another, and shook out their wet feathers.

Next morning I visited the lakeside again. The swallows were still there. At four o'clock in the afternoon I was sheltering from a heavy shower beside a low cherry tree, on which no flowers, or even buds, were apparent. In full view of me a pair of swallows flew in and alighted together on a branch scarcely higher than my head and about twelve feet from me. Their plumage was soaked, but they seemed happy and carried on a continuous conversation with low, melodious twittering. The next day all the travellers except a few stragglers had departed.

I have seen house martins alight on a dead tree in the Swiss Alps, but that was at mid-summer. It was remarkable to see the migrating swallows do so on this occasion without any hesitation; when the local swallows arrived later, they did not use these ready-made perching places. The migrants may have been Continental birds, for there was a touch of east in the high wind from the south, and this may have driven them off course. Indeed, the effect of adverse gales on bird migration had been evident in the Hebrides that autumn. Geese and whooper swans from Iceland had been contending with almost incessant storms during migration, and I had reports of geese flying north-west and north instead of south.

39

Writing of migrating swallows reminds me of a memorable experience I had on an early morning of early September many years ago. I had been judging the piping competitions at the Braemar Gathering all day and was expected to judge at the Kingussie Gathering on the following day. In order to do this it was necessary for me to cross the Cairngorms during the night. The distance from Braemar to Aviemore (which is near Kingussie) is twenty-eight miles, but I had road transport for only the first ten miles. The track through the Lairig Ghru is rough even in daylight, but the night was fine and I had reached the watershed at the Pools of Dee (2,800 feet above the sea) as the golden rays of the rising sun gilded the summit of Cairn Toul.

I was beginning the gradual descent on the Strathspey side of the pass, where cock ptarmigan were croaking among the screes, when I saw what appeared to be a serpent rapidly approaching me up the pass. Here is said to be the haunt of the Big Grey Man of Ben Macdhui. Fascinated, I stood still and watched, but only for a few seconds. The 'monster' was a flight of migrating swallows. They were flying south up the pass in a long line, and passed close to me. I had the rare experience of looking on them from above and admiring their dark blue backs, for they passed so low that they cannot have been more than two feet above ground-level. It is possible that the Lairig Ghru, since it cuts through the Cairngorm massif, may be a migration route for birds. At the Pools of Dee one April day, when the winter snow still lay hard and deep, I found a robin lying lifeless on the snow; it may have perished on migration in a blizzard.

Before the first world war, I was crossing a high pass in the Pyrenees in spring from Spain to France. On the lower ground the purple mountain saxifrage was already in flower, but as we approached the crest of the pass a blizzard of snow materialized, and, as we struggled against clouds of drift and a bitter north gale, I remember my French guide calling out to me: '*Fermez la bouche.*' He had no means of knowing that I was already familiar with blizzards on the Cairngorms in winter.

As we toiled upwards across the snowy wastes in frost and driven snow, I was astonished to see a swallow pass us, flying in zigzags up the pass less than a foot above the snow. It was remarkable that it was not blinded by the drift, but it had already reached the last few hundred feet of the ascent and would soon have passed beyond the snow line, after it had crossed the bleak and stormy frontier into France.

Great Pipers

A piper of renown said to me during the dark days of the second world war, 'There's one thing Hitler will never do; he will never stop the Pipes being played.'

No one can imagine Scotland without the highland bagpipe. There are more pipers now than there have ever been, and piping now appeals to a wider circle. Yet the piper lives in a changed world. It is next to impossible for him to give so much time to his art as it was in the days of the great pipers of the past. There are at least a score of splendid pipers of the younger generation, but I would not class any of them as outstanding, in the sense that the late John Mac-Donald of Inverness was outstanding in the Ceòl Mór or Great Music (usually called Pibroch), or as the late Pipe-Major George Maclennan was outstanding in the lighter music or Ceòl Beag. Nor is there anyone who can play the Competition March 'Bonnie Anne' like Pipe-Major William Ross, for many years the Piobaireachd Society's Instructor at Edinburgh Castle.

The mere fact of hearing John MacDonald play a Pibroch improved and stimulated a pupil's playing more than many lessons. My own tuition under him lasted eight years, and I treasure the memory of his playing as I heard it in his house in Inverness, on the Skye boat, on South Uist, in its old days of restfulness and peace, and also of course at the great Highland Gatherings, as some of my most uplifting experiences in a long life. The very perfection of his playing inspired the pupil to imitate him. John MacDonald was an intensely proud man and shunned publicity; it is a tragedy that the records he made (and they were few) are now unobtainable.

There is complete agreement among the pipers that the Classical Pipe Music ranks first—the Ceòl Mór. This has come down to us almost unchanged through the centuries; indeed the worthwhile compositions in Ceòl Mór written during the last hundred years can be numbered on the fingers of one hand. Some of the most noble and beautiful tunes in Ceòl Mór are those composed between 1600 and 1650. The great pipers of old memorized 100 to 150 compositions in Ceòl Mór. Each takes, on an average, 12–15 minutes to play, so the feat of memory was remarkable.

What is the definition of a truly great piper? His execution must be masterly—that goes without saying. His chanter reed and his drone reeds must be well balanced and melodious. But there is something, even beyond the perfect execution and the beauty of tone of his bagpipe, which distinguishes the great piper—it is his power to breathe life and beauty into the tune he is playing. He must live with his tune, and must be carried away by his playing.

One of the greatest pipers of thirty years ago was talking to me about the nervousness showed by some pipers in an important competition. He said that when he played in a competition he was carried away by the beauty of the tune he was playing. I gave the only answer which I think was possible; I said that I could well understand him being carried away by his playing, but that lesser mortals could not attain to that perfection, and were therefore nervous. A well-known amateur piper and piping judge told me years ago that he had just been having a lesson in Strathspey and Reel playing from that great teacher Pipe-Major William Ross. He said that when he attempted to emulate the swift and skilled execution of the Pipe-Major he could feel his own fingers 'crawling like elephants over the chanter'.

Of the celebrated pipers of twenty-five years ago there is but one who, at the age of ninety-three years, still keeps up his playing and that is Angus MacPherson, who can still call to life some of the old tunes and evoke the past glories of Ceòl Mór. Angus, who lost his home by the banks of the Shin in a disastrous fire, comes of a distinguished line of pipers. His father, Malcolm MacPherson, was a truly great player. Pipe-Major John MacDonald of Inverness (he was for a time Pipe-Major with the Cameron Highlanders) used to tell me that he owed much to his tuition by 'old Malcolm' who, in his opinion, was peerless as a player. Angus, therefore, from earliest childhood heard the pipes played by a master player, and all his long life his beautifully tuned bagpipe has been his companion. In 1969 he was honoured by the Queen at a special investiture at Balmoral Castle.

I suppose that each great piper has certain tunes in which he excels. John MacDonald's masterpieces were 'The Lament for Donald Ban MacCrimmon', 'Donald Duachal Mackay', 'The Earl of Antrim', and 'MacCrimmon's Sweetheart'; Pipe-Major Robert Reid, was, I always used to think, pre-eminent in 'Marion's Swan Song' and 'Lament for Mackintosh'.

Now that John MacDonald has departed, his greatness is shown by the number of pipers who claim to have been his pupils, but during his latter years John was able to play only on the practice chanter and not on the pipes, and Robert Brown and R. B. Nicol are among the very few who received tuition from the maestro when he was at the height of his musical powers. They made good use of this unique opportunity. During the autumn Pipe-Major Robert Brown illustrated for me a talk which I was asked to give on Classical Pipe Music before the Celtic Society of St Andrews University. It was a tribute to his outstanding playing that the large audience, most of whom had little knowledge of pipe music, remained interested for almost two hours, and at the close of the recital showed no disposition to disperse but lingered to ask questions and to congratulate the player.

One of the most memorable experiences in 1970 for the lover of the Ceòl Mór, the great music of the highland bagpipe, was at Boreraig in Skye, during MacCrimmon Day in Skye Week. Everyone knows that MacCrimmons for centuries were hereditary pipers to the MacLeods of Dunvegan. As master pipers they have gone, but the tunes they composed are still played by all celebrated pipers. Each year Dame Flora MacLeod of MacLeod crosses Loch Dunvegan to the MacCrimmon memorial standing high at Boreraig above the ruined MacCrimmon College of Piping. In the launch with her she has had for a number of years two of today's leading pipers, John MacFadyen and Seumas MacNeill, who is principal of the College of Piping in Glasgow. They play not only at the ceremony at the cairn but throughout the outward voyage of seven miles and during the return passage. This year the day was wet and stormy. The open launch was tossed by the waves, and it seemed impossible that the music should not be affected, yet we listened to one pibroch after another, faultlessly played.

This was only a prelude to the two tunes played beside the cairn— 'MacLeod's Controversy', played by Seumas MacNeill, and 'Lament for Mary MacLeod', played by John MacFadyen.

On the sea passage back to Dunvegan Castle a southerly gale was against us. John MacFadyen was playing at the bow when a wave broke over him. He continued playing as well as ever although the seawater, which had flowed down the drones of his bagpipe, for perhaps a minute altered their musical pitch. It was a memorable performance and one that would have been admired by the MacCrimmons who many a time in the chief's galley must have played under similar conditions.

Seumas MacNeill has done some excellent piping programmes on the radio and it is perhaps a pity that they are not broadcast more widely. One of our best players is still John MacFadyen. At the Glen Finnan Gathering, in difficult conditions with heavy rain, his playing of the pibroch 'Craigellachie', which is the gathering tune of the Grants, was outstanding. His brother, Iain, was second, for the fourth time running, at the MacCrimmon Silver Chanter competition at Dunvegan Castle, the winner of the Chanter being Hugh MacCallum, a player who has had much success since he won the gold medal at Inverness some years ago.

But the highlight of the season's piping was the playing, near the end of the competition at the Northern Meeting, of Donald Mac-Pherson. Donald, an engineer, lives at Exmouth, almost as far as he could be from the Highlands of Scotland. He has found it difficult to keep up his piping practice there and has not played, nor been present, at any competition during the past three years.

The Northern Meeting competition on the second day is open only for gold medallists—three years is a long time to be an absentee from competitive piping, and the genius of Donald MacPherson was in danger of being forgotten when, near the end of the competition in which there had been several good performances, he came quietly on to the platform. The judges asked him to play 'Lord Lovat's Lament'. The tune is unusual, full of music, one in which a great piper can be heard at his best. There was silence as Donald played. One variation glided into another in a flood of melody, the difficult grace notes played swiftly and lightly, the theme notes clear and bell-like. This was a performance that will live in the minds of all who heard it, a tune worth travelling miles to hear.

What of the future? Will Scotland be able to retain its pipe music at its former high level? Some of the older generation of pipers are inclined to be pessimistic, yet there are solid grounds for optimism. The College of Piping, which has its headquarters in Glasgow, has Seumas MacNeill as its Principal and John MacFadyen as its Secretary, and both can be depended upon to give a good account of themselves in the leading competitions. Classes are being held also in various places under the auspices of the Piobaireachd Society—for example Pipe-Major Nicol has on several occasions been teaching on the Outer Hebridean island of South Uist, where the talent for pipe music is outstanding. One summer I heard, in Skye, some of the pupils of the College of Piping, when General Martin of Husabost handed over to the College, for the annual rent of 'a Penny and a Pibroch', the site of the celebrated Mac-Crimmon College at Boreraig. The players I heard were, some of them, young lads, yet all played with assurance, skill and melody, and I am sure that if John MacDonald of Inverness had been present he would have been impressed and gratified by their performance.

A Golden Eagle Builds her Eyrie

I have studied the golden eagle of the Scottish Highlands for more than half a century, but it was only recently that I had the good fortune to see an eagle actually choose a new nesting site. I watched her and her mate carry in the first heather—and as we humans might put it, lay the foundation stone of the new home. Golden eagles are kingly and conservative birds. Most pairs own two eyries, indeed some are the owners of three, or even more, nests. The foundations of these eyries last, and there is thus no need to construct a complete new eyrie in the Arctic weather that goes by the name of spring in the Highlands and Islands. It is true that March may come in like the proverbial lamb, and the sun was warm that day as I began my watch near Creag na h-Iolaire, the Eagle's Rock.

That morning the female eagle, gliding low above the grassy rabbit-haunted slopes below the cliff, had climbed on the light east wind and disappeared in the distance. She returned, and alighted for thirty seconds on an eyrie she had built some years before. I imagined she had chosen that eyrie for her rearing of a family, but I was wrong. She rose and disappeared over the cliff-top, but almost at once reappeared, flying fast and straight towards the cliff face. Skilfully she avoided the crash-landing that seemed imminent and alighted on a ledge, placing in position the heather plant she was carrying. She rose, circled several times, then landed on the grassy slope 100 feet below the rock. Grasping a tussock of rough grass in one foot she dragged it from its root-hold, took wing, but dropped it before she reached the ledge on which she had laid the heather. She was evidently undecided, but as she stood there awhile as if thinking out a problem, she made her decision. After a short flight, she returned to the heathery ledge and began her task of nest-making. The new eyrie had as yet no shape; she settled down in a brooding position and began to scrape, turning on her breast as she did so. Slowly she hollowed out a nesting cup, all the time lying so flat on the nest that I could only just see her. Now and again, still prostrate, she scraped out the debris with her feet. It was hard work. She stood up, and rested for a few seconds. Then she flew fast, towards a neighbouring hill.

46

Her mate appeared and, tightly closing his wings, dropped several hundred feet in a display dive. Straightening out, he followed his mate at his best speed. The dark form of an eagle against the blue of a sunlit sky is a memorable picture, and was especially so on this occasion, with the young moon, white and cold in full daylight, as a background. Three days earlier I had seen the male eagle make a spectacular approach to the rock. A strong and stormy south wind was blowing and for a moment I saw a dark object falling headlong. Then the cliff hid him from view until he was almost overhead, and I saw him flying so fast that it seemed he must overshoot the nesting site. An exciting display of skilled diving followed. Moving at a speed of well over a mile a minute he suddenly closed his wings and fell headlong. Because he had been moving horizontally, at great speed, the dive was slanting rather than vertical—and the more breath-taking, because of this. It was almost exactly a year before that I saw the same eagle give an impressive flying display for the benefit of his mate as she stood near the top of the cliff. In quick succession he brilliantly accomplished one high aerial dive after another, then after each dive returning to his original height with quick, eager thrusts of his powerful wings. Still rising, he would suddenly close his wings tightly, his impetus causing him to rise still further in this unusual position. When his impetus was almost exhausted he would put his head down and skilfully use his tail to bring him into a diving position. At first he fell slowly, then faster and faster until, near the ground, he levelled off, using his travelling speed to aid the next upward flight.

The eagle is a heavy bird, and on a calm day this aerial display, one would think, must be tiring. The lady eagle also performs stunt flying and diving during the season of mating. On that very afternoon she visited her unfinished eyrie and then delighted me with a long spell of climbing and diving with great *joie de vivre*. Once, when half-way through her dive, she dropped into a tightly packed flock of starlings. At that distance the starlings seemed no larger than gnats as they scattered in alarm. The eagle shot through them as though they did not exist. She perhaps ignored them because birds of prey do not eat starlings unless really hungry: their flesh is not tasty.

Echoes from the Heights on Skye

It is perhaps from Elgol in the south of the Isle of Skye that the Cuillin Hills are most impressive, for they appear to rise almost sheer from the Atlantic. The most imposing peak is Garsven. Its high ridge falls away so sharply to a deep, dark corrie that the impression is given that half the hill has been crunched and bitten off by a giant's teeth.

As I watched Garsven on a sunny autumn day a small cloud, so thin that it was almost transparent, formed and lingered motionless close below the hill top. Suddenly, from the deep corrie that lay below slopes of scree, came the deep-throated roar of a stag. A broad arm of the Atlantic, Loch Scavaig by name, lay between me and Garsven; the sea here was calm as a mirror. North of Garsven rose needle-sharp peaks, Sgùrr Alasdair, Chief of the range, prominent among them. This peak commemorates Alasdair (Alexander) Nicolson, Sheriff of Skye, who, in the year 1873, was the first man to climb it. Beyond the farther shore of Loch Scavaig could be seen the dark waters of Loch Coruisk (Loch of the Corrie of Waters). Famous artists have painted it; great poets have written of its wild beauty. Sir Walter Scott described it as 'that stern, dread lake'. On Loch Coruisk are two small islands, on one of which a colony of Arctic terns nests. As yet, there is no road near the loch, and a moonlit night spent on its shore is a memorable experience. One day of early May a friend and I crossed the Cuillin from Glen Brittle by a high, very rough pass. In May the night is short and it was not until midnight that we saw the full moon reflected coldly in the dark, silent loch. On the shore we found a dead rowan tree, its stem and branches bleached by wind and sun, white and ghostly. With its wood we kindled a fire, and the smoke had a fragrance like incense—in keeping with the mysterious surroundings. The night was cold and we eagerly awaited the rising of the sun.

On our return journey a red deer hind was ahead of us on the pass. The climb became too difficult for her and she lay down in the shade of a rock, hoping we should not notice her as we passed. A little apart from the main Cuillin range is a lower yet formidable hill, Sgùrr na Stri, Hill of the Strife or Contention. In the past this hill formed the boundary between the lands of MacLeod of MacLeod and Mackinnon of Mackinnon. There is a tradition that a boy was taken to the top of that hill and was there 'thrashed within an inch of his life' in order that he should have deeply impressed on his mind the boundary agreed upon by the leading members of these two clans. South of Sgùrr na Stri, at Camusiunary, Bay of the Fair Shieling, is one of the loneliest houses in Skye, where a shepherd once lived and where the postman (a good walker) delivered mail once a week over the hill-pass. It was here that I listened to one of the most historic broadcasts in British history. The year was 1940, the time early summer, when the saga of Dunkirk was being enacted. As the Head Coast Watcher for Skye, I had walked nine miles through Glen Sligachan to appoint Lachlan Robertson, the Camusiunary shepherd, an Honorary Coast Watcher.

That day, windless, hot, and almost cloudless, is deeply impressed on my mind because that morning came the news that Viscount Fincastle, a companion on many expeditions, had been killed at Dunkirk, the only son of his heart-broken parents. Another well-loved son of Skye who gave his life for his country was Hamish MacDonald of Sleat, a man of great charm and courage. Towards the end of my long walk I had watched the birth of a small cloud on Garsven, a cloud so thin that the large stones on the hill face could be seen through it. That evening in the twilight at Camusiunary I listened to the voice of Winston Churchill telling the nation of the defeat at Dunkirk, but at the same time telling us all in his firm, inspiring voice, that the British nation would never give in. The peace and beauty of the surroundings in which that memorable broadcast was heard made it the more impressive.

Years passed, and now as I write thirty years later, when those born after our victory are in full manhood, there was sunshine on the high Cuillin, and again I was watching the birth of a small transparent cloud a little below the crest of Garsven. As my thoughts this autumn day were of this mysterious cloud, twice born in the same place, the deep silence was broken by the calling of wild geese on their migration. The travellers flew so high that they were unseen; their voices grew faint in the distance as they sped towards the south. Pink-footed and grey-lag geese regularly cross the Cuillin on their way south from Iceland; a friend of mine on one occasion saw them attacked, at a great height, by a pair of golden eagles—perhaps in play, for there were no casualties.

Sunset was near when, once more, came the roar of the invisible stag somewhere in the deep corrie of Garsven. Thrice the challenge was heard, strong and vibrant. That evening I measured the distance on the one-inch ordnance map. As the crow flies (perhaps one might here say the golden eagle) that stag's voice had carried a distance of three miles.

The Country of the Whooper Swan

After a night of frost the low February sun climbed slowly above snowy hills and shone on the small, west Highland loch where four pairs of whooper swans have made their winter home. They have chosen this loch because a small river flows through it, keeping part of the lochan ice-free except in very severe weather; another attraction is the water weed that provides them with a plentiful supply of food, easily obtained. Iceland is the summer home of most of the whooper swans which winter in Scotland.

They flight north-westward in spring and I remember the sunny morning late in March when I was watching the gannets flying low above the Sound of Harris as they returned from the Minch to their distant nesting stacks on the St Kilda group of islands. After a time I was at a loss for a few seconds to identify a party of large, white birds flying on the same course and very near the water. When they passed me I saw that they were migrating whooper swans, and that they were steering on the first land in that direction, which was Iceland. A cygnet in pale grey plumage accompanied the party, and I wondered if it had memories of its long southward flight the previous autumn when it crossed from its birth-place in Iceland on the flight of perhaps 800 miles to the west of Scotland, where it had wintered. Whooper cygnets usually remain with their parents during the first winter, but there are no cygnets with the four pairs of swans which I have recently had under observation.

It is thought that the west Highland golden eagles are now rearing few young because of a new and powerful pesticide in sheep-dip. It is possible that pesticides are influencing the fertility of the whooper swan also. The swans floated majestically on the dark water, their white plumage radiant in the sunlight. One pair was feeding near a reed-bed and as each bird in turn 'up ended', its strong bill, deeply submerged, tore out the hidden succulent weed on which it fed. In thick rushes a heron stood motionless at its patient fishing. One of the whooper swans suddenly noticed the heron (it is always unpopular in the bird world) and swam importantly towards it. The swan's atmosphere of authority and displeasure was not lost on the heron which moved more deeply into the reeds and anxiously watched the swan's movements for further signs of displeasure. A mallard drake was bolder, and as he swam confidently close to the swans, the green feathers on his head shone in the sunlight.

Where the loch was ice-bound a dipper stood on the rime-coated ice. Time and again it jumped into the water, swam and dived, for a minute and more, before returning to its chilly outlook station on the ice. At last its fishing was successful and it flew back with a silvery minnow in its bill. The prey was hammered with repeated ringing blows on the ice and then swallowed.

On a steep, narrow ridge at the edge of the snow-line high above the loch three stags were quietly grazing; they appeared to be poised dangerously on that narrow slope, although there was no wind and the sky was blue behind them. From where they fed they could see the great heather-covered rock where Prince Charles Edward Stuart was for a time concealed during his wanderings after the final Jacobite defeat at Culloden.

Nearer to the road is an historical landmark of a slightly later period. This has the name 'Johnson's Chair', and is the large stone on which Dr Samuel Johnson rested while on his journey with Boswell to the Hebrides in the late summer of 1773. It was here that the MacRaes (who were, and still are, the most numerous clan in the district) gathered round the two travellers, in the learned doctor's words, 'in considerable numbers, I believe without any evil intention, but with a very savage wildness of aspect and manner'. Johnson's Chair is fashioned by nature as a seat. It is known to few persons and has so far escaped vandalism. On their travels the two pioneers stayed with MacDonald of Sleat in Skye and Maclaine of Lochbuie in Mull. Lochbuie asked Dr Johnson if he was 'of the family of Johnston of Ardnamurchan'. Neither of the travellers apparently realized that he was honouring the doctor by inferring that he might be one of the stock of the great MacIain or Johnston of Ardnamurchan and Boswell had to explain that there was no 't' in Dr Johnson's name, and that he was an Englishman.

Long after the sun had set on the loch of the whooper swans the snowy slopes of the Sisters of Kintail were afire in his rays. Their colour, at first cold white, then golden, was, during the fleeting moments of sunset, an exquisite soft pink, warm and glowing.

Sgùrr Fhuarain, perhaps the most striking member of that high range, recalled to me the noble form of the Matterhorn on a lesser scale; like the Matterhorn it trailed a thin, diaphanous ribbon of cloud from its narrow summit where the golden eagle at times proudly surveys hill, glen and corrie. Let us remember that the celebrated Pibroch 'The Glen is Mine', was first played, beneath the Sisters of Kintail, by MacCrimmon its composer.

The Old Birch Tree

In the glens of the Cairngorms are to be found birches of great, sometimes almost incredible age. They are centuries old and their hollow trunks are on occasion the nesting places of goosanders. These venerable, inspiring birches growing, sometimes, in glens almost 2,000 feet above the distant sea, are late in responding to spring weather and the increasing heat of the sun; it is early June before they are in leaf. These trees are near the limit of tree growth in Scotland, yet their glens are sheltered, under ordinary conditions.

The gale which arrived one morning very early in mid-May was no ordinary storm. From the Outer Hebrides, where a wind speed of 100 miles an hour was recorded on the island of Benbecula, the hurricane crossed the Minch to the Isle of Skye, stripping the old trees which grow below Dunvegan Castle of their half-grown leaves, and injuring these trees so severely that they remained almost leafless all through the following summer. It can be appreciated that a wind of this velocity was not long in arriving in the area of the Cairngorms, 100 miles to the east, where perhaps the chief stronghold of the old native birch trees is to be found. That morning when the storm was at its height an unusually violent squall swooped down upon a side glen where one of these very old birches grew, and broke off the main stem (it showed no trace of decay) eight feet above the ground. Three weeks later I visited this unfrequented glen and saw the mortal blow inflicted upon this veteran of the forest. I had known that tree, and the chaffinches that sang from it, for sixty years, and its form and height during that long period.

Like the old Scots firs that grow near it, this birch tree had seemed as if endowed with eternal youth. Each year in June it had clothed itself with delicately perfumed leaves; the scent of those slow-opening leaves was indeed of exquisite fragrance. The tree, or most of it, now lay on the ground but, although violently severed from the roots, had stored sufficient food, and sap, to open the young leaf-buds. Their vitality, it is true, was lessened and had retarded them at least a fortnight compared with the undamaged leaves at the base of the tree. I had thus the rare experience of inhaling their retarded exquisite scent as they had their last few weeks of life.

Not all tree lovers know that the spring scent of the leaves of old birches in Highland glens is more than usually aromatic. This birch is now named *Betula verrucosa*, and is considered a distinct species from the weeping birch, the leaves of which have not quite the same scent. It may be remembered that in old days scent was distilled from the birch.

I thought of the changes in Highland wild life in the lifetime of this old fallen tree. In its youth the pine marten, and perhaps even the wolf, lived in this glen. The veteran Scots firs near it were never planted, but grew from natural regeneration, and this shows that the red deer was then a much scarcer animal than it is at the present time, when deer eat each seedling when it appears above the surrounding heather or grass. The kite (now extinct in Scotland) must often have sailed over it, for in my youth I was shown the remains of a kite's nest in the fir wood. One of the keepers in the district had good cause to remember those kites. He had forded the River Dee in order to fish a pool which fished better from the other bank. He took off his hose, leaving them on the bank and using his brogues as wading shoes. After fishing the pool several times he waded back across the river, to find no trace of his stockings. They were found, later in the year, forming a warm lining to the kite's nest. Kites were much shot in the Highlands because of the value of the feathers in their long forked tails. These were known to be almost indispensable in the tying of a salmon fly known as the 'Gordon'; it was told me that the last pair of kites on Upper Deeside were shot for their priceless feathers.

It is many years ago since I heard the story of a kite which lay, apparently lifeless, in a trap. The victim was released, its tail feathers were cut off, and the body was thrown carelessly on the ground. To the astonishment of its captor the kite suddenly came to life, spread its wings, and flew away. It had no tail to steer by, and its flight was erratic. Let us hope it survived, and grew a new tail. It is many years since the kite became extinct in the Highlands of Scotland, although it survives in Wales. The osprey and the sea eagle also became extinct. The osprey, thanks to the enthusiasm of the Royal Society for the Protection of Birds, is again nesting in Scotland and the same society is hoping to reintroduce the sea eagle.

The pine marten may have climbed the branches of the old birch of which I write. It was in the year 1889 that the last pair of pine martens were trapped in this area of the Cairngorms—a pair so old that their teeth had gradually been ground down during the years until only the stumps remained. They preyed mostly on rabbits, burying for future use those they could not eat.

Near the foot of the glen in which the ancient birch was struck down by the hurricane lives a deerstalker who is also a celebrated piper. He is one of the few persons now living who had the privilege of being a pupil of a renowned master piper of a past generation. His beauty of expression, combined with the nimbleness of his fingers, have won him all the great piping trophies, both at home and abroad. The red deer gather round his house without fear when he is playing, and in summer house-martins fly low over his house, under the broad eaves of which they nest. His wife has had the unique experience of feeding these house-martins on breadcrumbs which they are glad to have when the weather is too cold for insect life to be abroad.

The deer which feed fearlessly near the house have an ear for music. I have piped to them, and also to the grey seal, and the music of the bagpipe has brought both species near me. I hesitate to say that they enjoyed the music, but their interest in it overcame their natural fear of man.

As I write, the glen of the old birch is deeply buried beneath the first snows of winter. The house-martins are now catching insects in the hot sun of Africa with no thought of their summer home far to the north. In mid-May they will return to the long twilight evenings of early summer. Then the few remaining branches of the old birch will again drench the air with fragrance as chaffinch and redstart sing their songs on the high branches of surrounding trees, and nature renews her youth.

The Twin Boulders of Martin's Lift

On the high ground of Skye overlooking the old castle of Duntuilm are the crumbling walls of a ruined house, the home of the Martins of Bealach. The men of this celebrated Skye family had great physical strength—one of them engaged in mortal combat with the dreaded Each Uisge or Water Horse—but the most celebrated of the family was a man of letters, Martin Martin, whose book, *A Description of the Western Isles of Scotland*, published in 1703, is still a classic. In the year 1693 its author had the distinction of reading a paper before the Royal Society on the subject matter of this book, before its publication. Seventy years later the book was carried by Dr Samuel Johnson on his journey through the Hebrides with his friend Boswell. We know that before the year 1686 the author was governor or tutor to Sir Donald MacDonald of Sleat, who led his clan in 1688 at the Battle of Killiecrankie, and was 'out' in the first Jacobite rising of 1715. This book is of unique value as a record of Hebridean life and customs.

The October sun shone warmly on the old ruins. Near the shore, 300 feet below, a crofter was scything his small field of oats which had survived the rains and gales of the worst September in memory. Buzzards were rabbit-hunting; a pair of ravens appeared overhead, flying high and fast down wind. Each bird dipped in turn, and, a second later, uttered a single croak of satisfaction. Earlier that year a Hebridean thrush had sung his wild, strong song from a boulder near where I stood, and a handsome cock wheatear had hunted insects. South of the ruined dwelling, at a distance of 500 yards, two great boulders on the rough grass are spoken of locally as the 'Lift of Martin of Bealach'. No living man can lift either of them a single inch, but it is said that one of the Martins lifted one and placed it upon the other. In that position the great boulders rested for many years, perhaps for centuries. In course of time a shepherd of great strength succeeded in lifting the upper stone and dropping it to the ground. He failed to raise it again. At the present day the stones lie side by side, and are likely to remain thus until the end of time.

The old home of Martin of Bealach stands at the entrance to the

'Bealach', or Hill Pass, which descends to the low ground. It faces south and is sheltered from the north wind by a rocky slope, in April dotted with many bright flowers of the cushion pink. The view from here is inspiring in clear weather, and across the blue Minch rise the hills of Harris and South Lewis, the cone of their chief, named The Clisham, standing proudly above his neighbours. The Clisham was the only hill in the Outer Hebrides to have ptarmigan. Sixty years ago rabbits increased greatly on it and it was decided to let loose a number of ferrets on the hill to reduce them. The ferrets attacked the rabbits, but they found the ptarmigan a satisfying change of diet, and exterminated them. This was told me years ago by an old stalker on that ground and he was an intelligent observer of bird life. The stock of ptarmigan on The Clisham was, at the best, small and the area on which they lived was limited.

Nearly thirty miles across the Minch from Martin's ruin, both the south promontory of Harris and the tower of Saint Clement's Church at Rodil were clear. Here are the tombs of some of the MacLeod chiefs, for the family held lands in Harris as well as in Skye. Certain descendants of that great Skye poetess, Mary MacLeod, are sure that her grave is at Rodil, and not at Dunvegan in Skye. There is, I think, only one person living who knows the site of the grave. She is immortalized not only in her poems but in that moving MacCrimmon Pibroch, 'Lament for Mary MacLeod', played by the great pipers of the present day. Mary MacLeod lived to the age of 105 years. She was a blood relation of the chief and it is said that she was nurse to five MacLeod chiefs in her long life. She was banished to the rugged island of Scarba in Argyll because of a satire she composed on the chief, but was later brought home to Skye. In Gaelic her name is Mairi Nighean Alasdair Ruaidh, which means Mary Daughter of Red-haired Alexander.

As I looked across to Harris the north wind blew with a touch of winter in its breath. East, across a sea of deepest blue, rose the great hills of the north-west mainland—Slioch, An Teallach, Suilven and Canisp. These giants had already their first snow cover although the wild swans had not yet arrived from Iceland.

I might have hoped to see the unusual bird visitor which had appeared that autumn on the northern strip of Skye. It was a hoopoe, a bird usually associated with the sun-baked lands of the south of Europe. On its migration it had been blown far to the north and was lost. This wanderer showed little fear, often raising and lowering its crest as it hunted for grubs in the grass. Three hoopoes in recent years, to my personal knowledge, have arrived in the north-west of Scotland, and the Skye visitor was the fourth.

The sun set behind North Uist; colour faded from the sky and the new moon freed herself from the clouds and shone near the twin MacLeod Tables high above Dunvegan and its old castle.

Pink-feet in Perthshire

It was near sunset when my host and I made our way through a wood of tall, coniferous trees, capercaillie-haunted, to the shore of a loch. In an observation post we awaited the coming of the geese which each evening roost on the loch. It is only in comparatively recent years that geese have roosted here, but now they arrive each night in countless numbers, from October onwards.

There were already geese on the loch when we arrived. The last rays of the sun were lighting up the plumage of a long line of grey-lags, swimming near the opposite shore. In the centre of the loch were many mallard, and a few coots were swimming among them. The sun had scarcely set behind the snow-capped hills to the west when the clamour of approaching geese was heard. The birds came in from the north, in long lines and chevrons. As they neared the loch many of them fell headlong, as though out of control. Others planed swiftly down, their wings swept back, in close formation, like a squadron of fighter planes. They braked with whirring wings and made a skilled landing. These were pink-footed geese, of which the roosting population of the loch is chiefly composed.

Sunset merged into dusk, and still the main population delayed their coming. It was exciting to see the faint outline of approaching geese above the tall trees. On the horizon were small grey clouds, floating rather low and constantly changing shape, sometimes looking like geese. Occasionally a gaggle of grey-lags, heavier birds and apparently slower in flight, came in to alight. As dusk deepened geese arrived more frequently and in greater numbers. There was a babel of sound; the cries of incoming birds mingled with those already on the water. Now the mallard began to rise and flight swiftly out of sight. They usually make their departure when the arrival of the geese is at its height. The pink-feet were arriving from the south as well as the north. Those from the south flew lower and came in not far above our heads. The air was filled with a tumult of sound. A red grouse, appearing from nowhere, flew fast across the loch. Starlings flocked to their roosting trees. Some of the geese were now leaving the water and standing on the far grassy shore, beneath the trees.

By six o'clock it was reckoned that 5,000 geese had arrived. They had come from a large area, some from twenty or thirty miles away, others from only a mile or two. They feed on grass, and on the young autumn-sowed wheat, but the harm they do to young wheat and oats is more apparent than real. A farmer complained that his wheat had been cropped so close that nothing but the bare earth remained. But the farmer reaped a bumper crop, for the droppings had supplied valuable phosphates to the earth.

The pink-footed goose nests in large colonies in Iceland, as Peter Scott has recently shown, and it is probable that many Scottish birds are of this race. But there is also a large migration each autumn of Greenland-nesting pink-feet to Iceland, and thence for 700 miles to north and north-west Scotland. An apparent increase in the numbers of pink-footed goose is puzzling, because the barnacle goose is decreasing, and the habits of both species are not unlike. My own acquaintance with pink-footed geese at their nesting haunts was in neither Greenland nor Iceland, but in Spitsbergen.

It was at the end of June, and I was far up Gipps Valley, where the snow was melting and dry knolls were already snow-free. From one of these knolls a pair of pink-footed geese rose. The nest, containing two eggs, was lined with a little down. It was placed in the slight shelter of the low Arctic vegetation, which here consisted of the purple mountain saxifrage and *Dryas octopetala*, the creamy-white flowers of which had not yet opened. On this small knoll were the remains of no fewer than seven old nests, with old, broken eggshells in most of them, and the inference was that the same pair of geese had nested here for at least eight years. It is at least 1,500 miles from Spitsbergen to Scotland. The flight both ways would be 3,000 miles, probably more. In those eight years they would therefore have travelled at least 24,000 miles, and survived the dangers of blizzards, tempests and shot.

On 15th July on gently sloping tundra near the great Nordenskjöld Glacier in West Spitsbergen, a pair of pink-footed geese rose ahead of me, and showed great anxiety. Their nest was placed in a large plant of *Dryas octopetala*, the leaves growing green in the actual nesting cup, as though the goose had actually lined it with them. In a warm bed of pale-grey down were two white eggs, on the point of hatching, and a newly born gosling. The little fellow cheeped continuously, for it was feeling the cold despite its thick coat of greenish-yellow down. A third pink-footed goose's nest in Spitsbergen was built on a headland rising from the west coast. Here were nesting kittiwakes, Brünnich's guillemots and fulmars. White-winged snow-buntings flew over great snowfields, still unmelted in July.

Although it was near midnight and mist and gloom almost hid the headland, there was no darkness, for in Spitsbergen in summer the sun is high above the horizon throughout the twenty-four hours; indeed, the warmest hours were sometimes around midnight, when it was possible to bask in the sun's rays.

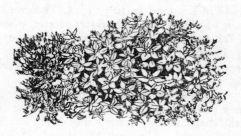

The Seven Men of Moidart

On the gently sloping shore of Loch Moidart, a secluded sea loch lying to the north of Ardnamurchan, in Argyllshire, are seven old beech trees, standing by themselves in a line. They are named the Seven Men of Moidart, and commemorate the seven gentlemen who accompanied Prince Charles Edward when he landed from France on the mainland of Scotland in July, 1745. The trees are growing in the neighbourhood of Kinloch Moidart House, where the Prince stayed 'for a full week', to quote from a contemporary account, before raising his standard at Glenfinnan. His stay at Kinloch Moidart is recorded in the names 'The Prince's Well' and 'The Prince's Walk'.

Who, it may be asked, are the Seven Men commemorated in these old trees? They were the Marquess of Tullibardine (he had been attainted for the share he took in the rising of 1715 and his younger brother now held the title of Duke of Atholl); Sir Thomas Sheridan, who had been tutor to the Prince; Sir John MacDonald, an officer in the Spanish service; Francis Strickland, an English gentleman; George Kelly, a clergyman; Aeneas (or Angus) MacDonald, a banker in Paris and brother of MacDonald of Kinloch Moidart; and O'Sullivan, an officer in the service of France.

The trees commemorating these men must be over 200 years old. The ground where they grow has little or no shelter, and it is therefore surprising that they should have grown into stately, spreading trees. But there is one tree in that carefully spaced line which seems as though it had been planted much later. According to the tradition of the neighbourhood this small tree is as old as the others but never prospered, as it was planted by one who later in the campaign was disloyal to the Prince. The inference seems to be that each tree was planted in person by the Seven Men of Moidart, and this indeed is likely, although I have seen nothing in writing to confirm it.

A year after the planting of the trees the Prince's cause had been finally lost on the field of Culloden and the inhabitants of Moidart were suffering for the part they had taken in the rising. Vengeance had been swift. MacDonald of Kinloch Moidart had been captured and hung and his head had been placed on view high above one of the gates of the city of Carlisle, where it remained for many years. The homes of his people had been plundered and then burnt; troops hunted men, women and children among the hills. Cattle were driven off or slaughtered. The house of MacDonald of Kinloch Moidart was set alight and burnt to the ground. The chief's mother, an old bedridden lady, was carried outside, and died beneath one of the old yew trees (one has recently been blown down) that for many centuries stood four-square and, like the yew at Fortingall, may have had a Druidic origin. The Prince had brought ruin and violent death to many, but the deeds of bravery and devotion that his coming had inspired will not be forgotten.

East and north-east from the shore of the sea loch beside which the Seven Men of Moidart spread their mighty branches to the autumn and winter gales, the hills rise steeply to the lonely boundary between them and the adjacent district of Lochailort. Two of the high hills that form the dividing line are Fros Bheinn (2,876 feet) and Sgùrr na Ba Glaise, Peak of the Grey Cow (2,817 feet). On a sunny day earlier in the autumn I had climbed from Lochailort to the watershed. The birches were still green and the blossom had not yet faded from the ling. It is a country that is still unspoilt, for no road leads from the low ground through Coire a' Bhuiridh, Corrie of the Roaring, where the raven croaks and the hoarse voices of challenging stags awaken the echoes on dark autumn nights. Ahead of me was the boulder-strewn peak of An Stac, where a covey of hardy ptarmigan have their home. Wisps of sea mist drifted in, white and ghostly, and at once the air temperature dropped, but rose again as the fog was dispersed by the warm sun. At the head of the corrie a steep, rock-flanked pass leads to the beckoning watershed. The sun could not reach this pass and the grass here, even at midday, was dew-drenched. At an elevation of rather more than 2,000 feet above sea level I passed a thriving colony of sea thrift; the red flowers had gone to seed, but it could be seen that they had been as tall and vigorous as those growing at sea level. For a few seconds a red deer, high above me, looked down from the crest of the pass. The steepness of the climb increased, and the stones half-hidden in the grass became more unstable.

The minutes dragged and the top of the pass seemed to be as elusive as ever. The air was cold and damp. Then, almost in a moment, I had reached the top of the pass and found warmth and sunshine and a view that recompensed me for much toil. I was less than 200 yards from a small herd of stags that were unaware of my presence. Some were feeding, others were lying drowsily near a spring on the sun-warmed slope. All the stags had imposing antlers and one was a 'royal'. More than 2,000 feet below me the sun sparkled on the small waves of Loch nan Lochan and on the dark firs that grew near it. No human figure had been in sight all that day; no aeroplane had sped across the blue depths of the sky. The peace and stillness of hill, glen and corrie had been unbroken; shafts of sunlight that evening increased the mystic beauty of the scene. The stags were still happy and unsuspicious when I left them.

Historic MacCrimmon Cairn

Each summer a Pibroch is played by a master piper at the high cairn which commemorates the great MacCrimmon pipers at the shore of Loch Dunvegan in sight of Dunvegan Castle in Skye. That cairn is comparatively recent, but on the mainland fifty miles distant, and almost unknown, is a very old cairn that bears Mac-Crimmon's name. The Gaelic name for the cairn is Carn Cloinn MhicCruimen, in English, Cairn of the MacCrimmon Clan. The cairn is on the summit of the hill named Glas Bheinn, and overlooks Skye, near the narrow sea strait of Kylerhea, which separates Skye from the Scottish mainland.

The district of Glenelg where this cairn stands was for centuries owned by the MacLeods of Dunvegan; the charter granted them by King David in the twelfth century was on condition that they provided a thirty-six-oared galley for the king at Kylerhea when he travelled between the mainland and the Isle of Skye. In the early years of the seventeenth century, Donald Mór MacCrimmon was MacLeod's piper at Dunvegan. He composed bold tunes, outstanding even among MacCrimmon compositions. As examples, let me mention two of them, 'MacLeod's Controversy' and 'MacLeod's Rowing Pibroch'.

Donald Mor had a brother living in the Glenelg district who went by the name Padruig Caog, in English Patrick of the Squint, because of a defect in an eye. He was excitable and had quarrelled with his foster-brother, some say a Matheson by name. One day after the quarrel, Patrick of the Squint was washing his face at a burn that was beside his thatched house when his foster-brother approached from behind and stabbed him fatally with his dirk. When news of this was brought to Donald Mór at Dunvegan he hurried to MacLeod's room and told his chief in grief and excitement that he was leaving at once on a mission of revenge. MacLeod succeeded in persuading him to wait for twelve months, thinking that the great piper's anger would have cooled by then. At the end of a year Donald Mór, telling no one of his intention, set out on foot for Glenelg. He found that his brother's killer was living in Kintail. Donald Mór collected his supporters in Glenelg and they crossed the hills to Kintail. They set fire to the village of the murderer, and burned eighteen houses with the loss of several lives. This rough justice is commemorated in the haunting Pibroch afterwards composed by Donald Mór. The tune has a strange name. Its Gaelic name is 'Lasan Phadruig Chaog', which may be translated, 'A Flame of Wrath for Patrick of the Squint'. The graves of those killed are traditionally said to be several hundred yards north of the cairn, on rather lower ground.

Donald Mór, knowing that his life would be in danger if he remained in the district, made his way to Sutherland, where he was for some years under the protection of the celebrated Donald Duachal Mackay, chief of his clan, who afterwards became Lord Reay. It is worth recording that in recent years, when the family papers at Dunrobin Castle in Sutherland were being examined, it was found that in the years 1624 and 1625 Sir Robert Gordon, as tutor to the minor Earl John of Sutherland, had entered in his accounts that he paid victual meal to 'Donald Maccrummin pyper', 20 bolls in 1624 and 13 bolls 2 firlots in 1625. It is possible, even likely, that the 'Donald Maccrummin' mentioned here is the same man whose great tunes, full of grandeur and vigour, are played, almost with veneration, by the great pipers of the present time. One of his compositions, 'MacLeod's Controversy', a unique and testing tune, was set at the Northern Meeting in Inverness in 1970, and was played with distinction by Neil Angus MacDonald from the Island of Barra.

The district where the old historic MacGrimmon Cairn stands, high above the strong tides of the Atlantic ebbing and flowing continuously through Kylerhea Sound, has many associations with the past. Here is situated Iomaire nam Fear Móra, Ridge of the Big Men, where, it is said, the Fingalians are buried. It is said that Reidh, one of the Feinne or Fingalians, attempted to vault the strait on his spear but failed and was drowned. The strait, it is said, is named after him. In the 'Old statistical Account of Scotland' the Reverend Doctor Beith, Minister of Glenelg, writes in the year 1841:

> Superstition had for long attached sacredness to this spot and predicted all manner of wrath to the intruder who would lay unhallowed hands upon it. About 70 years ago (1771) however, a number of gentlemen belonging to the district resolved to brave the danger and put the tradition to the test.
>
> They selected a cloudless day in August, and set to work to open the mounds. They had not gone very far when they came

upon two sarcophagi, formed of large flags, containing the remains of skeletons of the most extraordinary size. An eye-witness stated that when the under jaw-bone of one of the skeletons was placed round the lower face of a very large and stout man present, it could so be held without touching him, being at the extreme parts nearly two inches apart.

They were in the act of replacing the jaw-bones when suddenly the sky, which up till now had been very bright, got overcast, and a tremendous storm burst upon them. They replaced everything as quickly as they could, threw in the earth and made for home as if the ghosts of MacReath and the Fingalian warriors were at their heels.

It is in the neighbourhood of the Ridge of the Big Men that Glen Bernera leads towards the broad, rocky dome of Glas Bheinn and the MacCrimmon Cairn. The midsummer sun was strong, and the scent of new-mown hay was in the air as we made our way up the glen towards the hill. Past Eas Mór, the Great Waterfall, thin after weeks of drought, we walked, and at the head of the glen found ourselves near the boundary between Inverness-shire and Ross-shire. Below us to the north-west was Teanga na Comhstri, the Tongue of Contention. The 'Tongue' is a heathery slope rather more than 100 yards in width, between two small burns falling into the sea strait. It was claimed by the two counties for centuries, although without value, as far as can be seen.

Although almost at the hill top, the MacCrimmon Cairn is not visible until the climber is close to it. It was disappointing to find that the stones of this historic cairn had been scattered and that an unsightly and cemented 'triangulation mark' had been built at its very core during the last Ordnance Survey of the Highland hills. Had the historic value of the cairn been realized it would have been easy to leave it and build the 'triangulation mark' a few yards away, as the ground is almost level.

The Ospreys Grow Up

The return of the ospreys to nest successfully on a Scots fir on Strathspey in 1959 marked the beginning of a remarkable record of success by the Royal Society for the Protection of Birds in osprey protection. The osprey, handsome, inoffensive, living entirely on fish, nested in Scotland 100 years ago. It was shot and the eggs were taken in the days long before bird conservation was thought of, and by the early years of the present century had been wiped out as a nesting species in Scotland. The species continued to nest successfully in Sweden and Finland and it is possible that a pair from that area when they passed over Strathspey on their northward migration in spring, seeing an area that resembled their homeland, decided to nest here. They built an eyrie, indeed several eyries, but their eggs were taken from them, for a Scottish-taken osprey's egg reached a fantastic price.

Then in the year 1958 the Royal Society for the Protection of Birds began the Operation Osprey. The first year despite a careful watch the eggs were taken on the exceptionally dark and misty night of June 3rd, but since then a remarkable series of successful seasons still continue as I write in the autumn of 1970. During the twelve seasons beginning in 1959, a twenty-four-hour watch has been mounted immediately the ospreys arrive (the male usually arrives several days before the female). The only unsuccessful years were 1963 and 1966—in each of these the nest and eggs were destroyed by a gale. In each of the other seasons young have been successfully hatched and reared. For this happy result, Mr George Waterston, the Scottish Representative of the Society, and a team of enthusiastic helpers deserve the thanks and admiration of all bird lovers. I was indebted to the Royal Society for the Protection of Birds for the use of their forward hide in making the observations recorded.

The eyrie is on the crown of an old Scots fir growing on a small dry knoll in typical greenshank country, where on much of the spongy, acid ground, old trees scarcely the height of a man have a struggle to maintain life. The osprey's tree, growing on drier ground, is higher than most. During my first watch the young ospreys, hatched about ten days before, were still in down, chocolate-brown

70

on the head and white on the back. The father of the family brought all the food; the mother never fished and was almost continuously at the nest. The prey consisted, without exception, of fish. One large sea-trout was brought in, but most of the fish were brown trout weighing from about $\frac{1}{2}$ lb. to $1\frac{1}{2}$ lbs.

Three weeks later, when I again saw the eyrie, there was a remarkable change in the young. They were full-feathered, and had even grown the characteristic crest. On 26th July, excited by a strong wind from the south-east, the most forward of the young birds was flapping its wings vigorously and jumping from the eyrie almost a foot into the air. I could see the pale edgings to the feathers of the neck and mantle, absent in the parent birds; otherwise there was little to distinguish the young from the adults.

The female osprey left the nest during my watch, sailed overhead and then, in full flight, broke off a branch from a lifeless, bleached fir, carried it back and carefully built it into the eyrie. All the branches, brought by cock or hen, were broken off in flight and their sharp crack could be heard. The female watched intently as a pair of swifts approached the nest against the wind. The male appeared, carrying a fish whose amber fins glistened in the sun. He laid it in the eyrie, then flew to his usual perch on a neighbouring dead tree.

One evening I looked upon a snowy shore of white water-lilies almost girdling Loch Mallachaidh, Loch of the Curse. The stream which flows from this loch is of ill-omen, especially to newly married couples: it was considered unlucky to cross it on one's wedding day. For a moment, I thought the osprey was approaching me to fish, but the bird which passed overhead in the fading light was a greater black-backed gull. There is, indeed, a gull-like quality at times in the flight of the osprey, but it often reminded me of the black kite, which my wife and I watched on the Lake of Geneva.

Later that evening I returned to the osprey hide. Herring gulls were slanting in from the east. The high tops of the Cairngorms were hidden in cloud. At 8.20 the male osprey set out on his evening fishing expedition, his flight westward as usual rather low above the dark pines. Midges had eagerly invaded the hide before I left in gathering rain.

Three days later, prolonged rain was ending as I approached the osprey country. The air was calm, and each pine needle glistened as its pendulous raindrop caught the light. The effect on the forest was as if a light snow-shower had fallen. At noon the male osprey left his dead and whitened tree and set out for the invisible Spey. He had previously flown in twice, at very short intervals, each time with moss in one foot. The female had perched, high and prominent, on the eyrie's edge, preening: in the same position stood her largest nestling, also crested, the pale-edged mantle and wings distinguishing it from its parent.

The male returned with a fish at one o'clock. The strong light shone on his crest and his white breast, mottled with brown, as he prepared to alight. There was then much activity in the eyrie, the female osprey feeding the young, and both male and female carrying in pine branches, some of considerable size. I could only think how different would have been the golden eagle's behaviour at this stage. The male eagle would have arrived with prey, and, having left it in the nest, would almost at once have taken wing, leaving the eaglet to pluck and eat as best it could.

Later, after chasing off a carrion crow, the female osprey continued to repair the eyrie, perhaps because it had suffered from the prolonged rain. The young ospreys were doing most vigorous and excited wing exercises, one of them for a moment becoming completely airborne and rising perhaps a couple of feet into the air. It held on, during its wing-flapping, to small pine branches, loose in the eyrie, apparently to act as ballast. The mother brought from the moor a very large ball of moss. When she placed it on the floor of the eyrie, she had difficulty in freeing her claws of it.

At four o'clock I saw, for little more than a second, the male pass a dead pine some distance away, carrying a fat trout of perhaps a pound in weight. When he disappeared from view, I expected him to arrive within a minute at the eyrie, but had to wait three-quarters of an hour before he came. He had evidently been in the female's view, for she had often called. In the interval the male had clearly been feeding on the trout, for when he brought it in, there was scarcely more than half the fish left—the head and shoulder had been entirely eaten. The female picked up the trout, carried it to a dead tree, and daintily fed on it.

After five minutes she climbed into the air a considerable distance, then flew in with the trout, alighting, eagle-like, at the eyrie and at once offering small morsels to the smallest chick. Big Brother meanwhile indulged in strenuous wing exercises with tail held fan-shape. He faced the chilly north-east breeze and the low clouds, which brought a sharp and sudden shower, through which a wandering roe deer barked hoarsely.

My last morning (30th July) in the hide was calm and grey. The strongest of the three young ospreys watched, with interest, a swift and, later, seagulls flying high overhead. He then began his usual

F

wing exercises and lifted a few inches above the floor of the eyrie a small stick perhaps six inches long. Suddenly he rose almost vertically into the air and hovered over the eyrie in masterly fashion, keeping station perhaps six feet above the floor of the nest. The remarkable thing was that he carried out this operation perfectly, as a helicopter might have done; with less skill and precision he might easily have flown beyond the eyrie, on to which he now made an easy landing. The first hover-flight of a young osprey was a thrilling sight. I doubt whether the young of any other species rise vertically from the nest and return thus to it on a first flight.

A little later the father came in with a large dead branch held in one foot. As he placed it in the eyrie, he actually alighted on it while still partially airborne, beating his wings to lessen his weight. Male and female flew off side by side. Flying thus, they gave a display, dropping and retracting legs and talons. An hour and a half later, the male was seen with a large trout. As he stood on a dead tree, I could, through my glass, see him eating the shoulder of the fish. The trout was still alive, and occasionally flapped its tail feebly.

The young ospreys would soon leave their sanctuary and face the dangers which beset all birds of prey from the man with the gun. Do the parents accompany the brood and teach them how to fish? Observations such as these would be welcome from nature observers.

No Snow on Braeriach

Is there perpetual snow in Scotland? That is an interesting question often asked. There are snow-beds on several Scottish hills which remain unmelted through most summers. On one of the rare summer days when the shade temperature in Fort William stands at 80 degrees Fahrenheit, the great snow-bed in the north-east corrie of Ben Nevis can be seen from the main road near Inverlochy Castle on a sweltering day of July or August. There is indeed a local saying, 'Lochiel will hold his lands so long as there is snow on the Ben'. The Macintyres of Glen Nodha paid their rent, on Midsummer's Day, of a 'white-fatted calf, and a bucket of snow' taken from a high corrie of Cruachan Beann above Loch Etive. The Munros of Foulis for centuries have held their lands on condition that they 'supplied a bucket of snow at the Palace of Holyroodhouse on Mid-summer Day to cool the King's wine'. The Munros of Foulis were able to supply this snow because on Ben Wyvis, which rises near their ancestral home, snow lies in a gully until late summer, some-times throughout the year. Ben Wyvis is the modern spelling of Beinn Uais, the Noble Hill; in late spring when it carries a great depth of snow it is truly Alpine. The Grants of Rothiemurchus, whose land on the Cairngorm Hills reaches a height of 4,248 feet above the sea, have a tradition that they hold their land on con-dition that they supply the sovereign with a bucket of snow whenever this is asked for.

The snow-bed on Braeriach, which is the subject of this chapter, is almost within a stone's throw of the lands of Rothiemurchus but is just over the watershed and actually is in the Deer Forest of Mar, for long held by the MacDuffs. I have made observations on this snowfield in autumn, when it is at its lowest ebb, for more than half a century, and the only occasion I have seen it entirely dis-appear was in 1959. That summer in the Central Highlands of Scotland was the warmest in living memory. In early September that year, I made an expedition to the site of this snow, which lies in one of the most remote areas of the Cairngorm Hills, near the boundary or 'march' between three great deer forests, Rothie-murchus, Mar and Glen Feshie.

It was a strange experience to be on the high hills in late summer with no lessening of the heat. The sky was cloudless; the heather bloom, even at 2,500 feet above the sea, was completely over and almost lifeless from the drought, although on the north-west coast two days earlier, almost at sea level, the blossom was still fragrant. The exceptional character of the season was shown by the second flowering of Alpine plants. At 2,500 feet above the sea there were red buds and pink china-like flowers on *Azalea procumbens* and at 3,500 feet a plant of cushion pink (*Silene acaulis*) carried a red flower, perfectly formed. In the spray of the burns were golden blooms of the mountain species of the marsh marigold, which I had never before seen in full flower in September. It was strange also to find that the water of these hill streams, usually ice-cold, was comparatively warm.

The Braeriach snow-bed lies at the west face of a wild and deep corrie known as An Garbh Choire, in English, the Rough Corrie. It is approximately 3,800 feet above the sea and is immediately below a sheer precipice 200 feet high, which falls from the summit plateau of Braeriach. The snow is drifted in here, on westerly blizzards, to a great depth during the winter months. In summer it is sheltered from the warm winds and, during most of the day, from the sun. In late summer it becomes almost solid ice, and it has been suggested that this may be the site of the last British glacier. In autumn the snow splits into several 'pockets' which become discoloured by fine gravel and peat dust and might escape notice from the Lairig Ghru Pass, one of the few places from which this snow is visible. When I was on the pass this September morning I was surprised to see that, for the first time in my life, there was no snow visible in the corrie. It was incredible, but, in order to make doubly sure, Morag the cairn terrier (she felt the unusual heat even more than I did) and I set out on the long and latterly steep climb over unstable boulders and 'screes' to the site of the snow, the sun beating down with tropical heat.

As we approached our destination I realized how exceptional were the conditions that year. In the 'screes' the attractive parsley fern had grown fresh young leaves and the hill grass was green as in early summer. The starry saxifrage was flowering a second time, and the seeds of the alpine cudweed (*Gnaphalium supinum*) in places formed a white carpet on the ground. At length we had climbed to the base of the precipice and stood where the snow should have been lying. It had gone, completely and without trace and, more remarkable, it had disappeared two months before it could have been reinforced by the arrival of the first autumn snow. Gone were the small streams from the snow which usually moisten the ground beneath them. Instead of being soft and damp, it was dry, and even dusty. It was interesting to notice how the character of the vegetation changed as one approached the 'pockets' which usually hold the last of the snow in late summer. Of phanerogams, or flowering plants, *Saxifraga stellaris* approached the snowy zone most closely. (I have noticed that this is also the case in the snowy corrie of Ben Nevis.) Still nearer to the 'pockets', mosses, bright green and full of life, were beginning to grow. Even they stopped short where, certainly for twenty-five years, the snow had remained, summer and winter. The rocks themselves were clean and bright as though newly quarried. It was by now early afternoon, and already the fierce sun was hidden by the precipice above, and the air was cool.

The absence of bird life, throughout that long day's walk of fourteen hours, was remarkable. The stock of ptarmigan that year was at a low ebb: I did not see one ptarmigan, or one grouse, all day. No soaring golden eagle cheered me, nor a white-winged snow-bunting. The one bird I did see was a meadow pipit.

At half past six that evening, when I crossed the young Dee a short distance above its junction with the stream known as Allt Garbhchoire, the sun was setting behind the precipice of Braeriach above the site of the snow-bed I had visited. As the upper rim of the sun disappeared, glowing and quivering, a shaft of light shot into the sky towards the stony slopes of Cairntoul. While I walked south by Lairig Ghru near the clear River Dee, the sun bathed the high inhospitable dome of Ben MacDhui (4,300 feet) in a delicate pink glow, and the rocks on dark Carn a' Mhaim became burnished gold. This was a truly alpine scene, and in the evening light the marks of a recent cloudburst high on the face of Coire Bhrochain of Braeriach became still more conspicuous. Low in the southern sky the young moon now contended with the sunset. The path became indistinct as I crossed the shoulder of Carn a' Mhaim and ahead of, and rather below me, saw the old firs of the Robbers' Thicket. Fourteen hours earlier I had watched the morning light hill and glen here. Now the moon was setting and a star shone near the zenith. A chill air drifted up from the river. The track was now almost invisible and progress slow. Of Morag there had for long been no sign. I realized how much the moon had meant to me earlier as I now searched for my car which I had earlier left near the stalker's cottage at Luibeg, last outpost of Mar Forest. The car at length loomed out of the blackness only a few feet from me—and there, hopefully awaiting me, sat Morag.

That expedition was in the year 1959, and the snow certainly remained unmelted, summer and winter, for the next ten years.

Fairies in the

The Gruagach or Long Haired One (from the Gaelic *gruag*, a wig) is, according to tradition, a fairy who has intimate association with the Isles of the Hebrides. This sprite might be of either sex, but was usually in the form of a woman; the hair was always long and flowing. He or she tended the cattle and prevented them from falling over the rocks or into the moorland bogs so prevalent in the Hebrides. In return for these services an offering of milk was expected at night.

In the neighbourhood of a number of Hebridean communities Clach na Gruagach, the Gruagach Stone, is still to be seen. The stone always has a hollow in it, and after the last of the evening milking the hollow in the stone, usually a rounded one, was filled with milk for the Gruagach. Unless this was done the cows would, it was believed, yield no milk at their next milking, or the cream would not rise to the surface of the milk.

In some districts the tradition is that milk was placed in the Gruagach Stone only when the people were going up to, or returning from, the summer pastures. Martin Martin, writing about 1700, mentions that on the island of Vallay, which at low tide is joined by a smooth, wet strand to North Uist, below the three chapels which were still to be seen in his day, was 'a flat, thin Stone, called Brownies Stone, upon which the ancient Inhabitants offered a Cow's Milk every Sunday, but this Custom is now quite abolish'd.' Thus it seems that a daily offering was not essential.

Dr Samuel Johnson, who with Boswell visited Skye in 1773, writes of the Gruagach as follows: 'In Troda (an island lying off the north of Skye) within these three-and-thirty years, milk was put every Saturday for Greogach, or the Old Man with the Long Beard. Whether Greogach was courted as kind, or dreaded as terrible, whether they meant, by giving him the milk, to obtain good, or avert evil, I was not informed. The Minister is now living by whom the practice was abolished.'

The island of which Johnson writes had the reputation of being haunted, and at least one family who had meant to settle there left in dismay because of the unearthly shrieks and cries heard when

79

darkness had fallen. Storm petrels nest on the island, and their cries, uttered on the wing in darkness, have an eerie quality which might well strike terror into the hearts of the credulous and superstitious.

The Gruagach was usually a friendly sprite, but at times was resen\` ul of an insult. A woman of Scorrybreck in Skye, it is said, was trying to drive her cows into the byre while the family Gruagach, with puckish perversity, kept them out. The woman's temper flared up, and she cursed the fairy, who retaliated by slapping her on the cheek with such violence that she died. All the same, this Gruagach (he was a male) kept the peat fire going all that night for the woman who sat up watching the body.

There are perhaps more Gruagach Stones in the Isle of Skye than elsewhere. At least three, and probably more, exist on the north-east wing of that island—at Scorrybreck, Holm, and at Digg, not far from Flodigarry, where at one time Flora MacDonald, preserver of Prince Charles Edward Stuart, had her home.

Brunaidh, or Brownie, seems to have been the Gruagach under another name. The name 'Brownie' apparently came to the Hebrides from the Lowlands of Scotland. One of the most celebrated Brownies lived on the small island of Cara, near the Isle of Gigha, off the Kintyre peninsula. For centuries Cara has been owned by the MacDonalds of Largie, and it is said that no MacDonald sees eye to eye with a Campbell. Kenneth MacLeod, the celebrated folk-lorist and collector of Gaelic songs, took me over the strait from Gigha, where he was at the time Parish Minister, and showed me the Brownie Stone of Cara. As it happened, we crossed the sound while an eclipse of the sun was taking place, and the wind freshened as dusk replaced the noon sunshine; my guide told me, in his own vivid and inimitable fashion, of the Brownie's dislike for the hated enemies of the MacDonalds, the powerful Clan Diarmid. Indeed, he said, the Brownie would permit no Campbell to land on his island. He, the Minister, had once crossed with a Campbell, and had not remembered this until they were at sea.

'What did you do?' I asked him.

He replied, 'It was quite simple; I made a small cut in his finger and let out a drop of his Campbell blood. This satisfied the Brownie and no obstacle was placed in our way when landing on Cara.'

The Cara Brownie was said to have kind feelings for most mortals. He put the island house in order before the arrival of visitors, and was of scrupulously clean habits, but he disliked dogs being left in the house at night, and at times killed those which had not been put out. Those humans not of tidy habits received hard slaps in the dark, slaps so violent that the skin was blackened and bruised. His kindly side is shown in the tradition that on the Brownie's Stone on Cara the visitor may obtain his or her most cherished wish.

The three tutelary beings of the Celts were Gruagach, Brunaidh and Glaistig, the last a small woman with yellow hair 'reaching to her heels'. Some say that she was a woman of the human race, placed under spells. Her dress, like the fairy's dress, was green. It was on account of the paleness of her face that the name Glaistig was given to her, *glas* being Gaelic for grey. One of the MacIains of Ardnamurchan, because of his kindness to a Glaistig who was once hungry, had a large byre miraculously stocked with cattle. On the death of Mac Iain Ghiarr, as he was named, this Glaistig roused the echoes on Ben Resipol in Ardnamurchan with her grief. The same night she was seen on the Cuillin hills of Skye, but never again.

One of the names given to the Glaistig was Gruagach Sheombair, or Housemaid, for during the night she swept the floor, arranged the furniture and sometimes spun throughout the dark hours. She too, was said to care for cattle and would accompany them to the summer pastures. In old days the inhabitants of the Western Highlands and Islands had small thatched dwellings in the hills. In May the people and their cattle went up to the shielings (this custom is still followed in Switzerland) and remained during the summer in order that the grass of their homelands might be rested. As a reward for the Glaistig who had helped them on their journey, milk was poured out for her each evening into the hollow of a special stone. Whether Glaistig and Gruagach were on occasion both present, and whether they then shared the milk, we are not told.

Rising Waters and the Divers

The Highlands of Scotland, especially towards the west and north-west, are the summer haunt of that large handsome bird, the black-throated diver; in winter the ocean is its home, to the Bay of Biscay and even farther south. The true divers (to which also belong the great northern, and the red-throated) have their legs set far back and can walk only with difficulty. They therefore lay their eggs so near the water that the brooding bird can dive from its nest, usually placed on an island of a freshwater loch, and swim away submerged. Such a nesting site has its disadvantages: the loch may rise after rain and float the eggs away. This indeed happens regularly.

Last summer, for example, a pair of black-throated divers nested on an island in early May. A flood removed the eggs. A second clutch also met with disaster. No one in the district had known the divers to lay a third time, and the interest of the ghillies, who rowed the anglers fishing the loch, was aroused when, in July, the diver was seen again prospecting her island. In mid-July a third clutch was laid and everyone hoped that they would be hatched. Alas, once again the waters of the loch rose and the eggs were washed away.

A stalker friend of mine, who is a reliable observer, has his home near a grassy islet where a pair of black-throats nest. Some years ago, I visited him on 28th June. The diver was sitting on two eggs. My friend told me that on 18th June the loch had risen rapidly, and a smaller islet, about 90 feet distant from that on which she was brooding on 28th June, and which was her earlier nesting place, disappeared beneath the waves. Two days later, my friend noticed that the diver was brooding on the larger island, and he and I agreed that in two days she could not possibly have laid a second clutch. She must, therefore, have in some way moved the eggs from one island to the other and have coaxed them up the shore.

The season before I had watched a black-throated diver in her efforts to save her egg from a rising flood. The egg was on a rushy promontory in sight of a fishing lodge. My friends and I were having tea when the diver appeared and began to build up with rushes the side of her nest nearest the water. As she brooded she snipped off rushes with her bill and laid them by her side. On one of the party appearing at the door of the lodge, the bird crouched on the nest, then dived. She was soon back, and continued to build a breakwater of rushes beside her nest.

Then, as the loch continued to rise, she lay awash in the shallow water, and broke off rushes and other plants *below* the surface. When she was obliged to swim because of the increasing depth of water, she snipped off green rushes with her bill and threw them over her shoulder. The wind drifted them towards the nesting cup, and she may have had a vague idea that they would form a breakwater to protect the nest. A fresh egg sinks, and the next day her egg was lying abandoned in several inches of water. I then gathered and weighed the rushes which the diver had collected to protect the nest. They weighed just 3 lb. The stems were cleanly cut, as if with a knife, and the cuts were diagonal. This behaviour was the more remarkable as the diver normally makes no nest.

Although last summer was unfortunate for one pair of divers, a pair from a neighbouring loch was successful in their nesting, for five birds were seen together in September. It is then that the parent divers prepare for their departure to the Atlantic. They often fly to the sea to fish, even in early summer, and on one occasion a diver dropped a herring of 1 lb. as it flew near its sitting mate. But this annual autumn seaward flight is a serious event in the life of these birds. One September evening the owner of the forest and the head stalker were still on the high ground after a day on the hill. The air was mild and still, and a strange and powerful clamour was wafted up to them from the loch far below and already indistinct in the shades of approaching night. This was the excited discussion which each year is carried on by the divers the evening before their departure. The next morning the birds had gone; they had exchanged the small waves of their loch for the ocean swell.

The black-throated diver is one of the most exciting and beautiful birds in the Scottish Highlands, and it is only occasionally that complaints are voiced about the harm it does to the stock of trout. One of the best sea-trout lochs in the Highlands is the spring and summer home of two pairs of divers, which are seen daily on the loch from March to September. They have been here from time immemorial, yet the stock of sea-trout shows a steady increase.

The 'Highlands' of Switzerland

In Britain the alpine swift is rare, and its appearance is a great thrill for ornithologists, for it is an exciting bird, larger than the common swift and even faster in its flight. It is easily distinguishable from our common swift by its larger size, pale brown upper parts and white breast and belly. One of its unusual appearances in this country was when a flight of nine entered a bedroom of a house in Kent, overlooking the English Channel, on 16th May 1916. This was during an intense period in the first world war, and it is possible that the birds were disturbed and bewildered by the shattering cannonade.

One of the largest colonies in Europe of the alpine swift—it consisted that summer of 169 pairs—is in the round tower of the old Jesuit church at Solothurn in Switzerland. Here careful and minute observations on the birds' breeding habits have been made, over many years, by a local naturalist, Herr Hans Arn-Willi, to whom my wife and I were indebted for a memorable evening high up in the interior of this church, which dates from 1689. The cold weather experienced that year in Switzerland during May and the first three weeks of June slowed down the nesting cycle of the swifts, one or two of which actually succumbed to hunger and cold. At the time of our visit, on 25th June, not all the birds had laid, although neighbouring nests held broods of different ages. One bird had been brooding closely for four days, yet she had not laid her first egg. The usual number of eggs in a clutch is three, but that year, because of the scarcity of food, clutches of two were usual. The eggs are rather large, white and polished, and very elongated. Most of the nests are built on the floor of the tower just inside the eaves. They are small and neat and are made almost entirely of the sticky bud-cases of the beech, which are blown from the branches of the trees and are caught in mid-air by the swifts. The adhesive quality of the bud-cases is heightened by the glutinous saliva of the birds, and the result is a nest that will last for years. It might be thought that the wall of the nest, when dry, would be brittle; actually it is almost like rubber, and Herr Arn-Willi showed us that the saucer-like nest could be bent with considerable force and vigour without harm.

It was a memorable experience, seated in a small observation post in the twilight of the ancient tower, to await at sunset the arrival of the alpine swifts. During our wait we learned interesting facts from Herr Arn-Willi. It was unexpected to be told that the birds arrive from Africa almost, sometimes quite, a month earlier than the common swift. That year the first bird was seen on 29th March. The young leave in September and the parents not until early October. The parents remain, therefore, at their summer haunts for six months, whereas the common swift's stay is little more than three months. Herr Arn-Willi believes this is due to the alpine swift's love of sleep. He has found that, even at mid-summer, they roost for approximately twelve hours. The young, being fed for a fewer number of hours each day, grow more slowly. Careful investigations show that they remain in the nest for eight weeks.

About seven o'clock in the evening alpine swifts began to appear at small holes under the eaves, alighting noiselessly and remaining a few seconds before going to their nests. Those that had brought insects for their young arrived with their pouches full of food—food captured perhaps on the slopes of the Alps on the far horizon. One little company consisted of seven pairs; some of the nests were actually touching. The new arrivals took up their roosting stations clinging to the wall, but two birds rested on a cross-beam, close together like love birds. When the swifts descended into the interior of the building, to their roosting stations a few feet below the eaves, they did so diagonally, creeping down with their claws gripping the walls. The alpine swift has remarkable claws. When a young bird is lifted from the nest, even before it is feathered, it clings to the human finger and even when held upside down maintains its grip.

The intimate acquaintance of Herr Arn-Willi with the individual swifts of the colony was shown when he took us to see a bird brooding on her eggs. When he attempted to push her off the nest she attacked his hand angrily. He said that this was the only bird in the whole colony to show fight when disturbed in this way.

The first record of this alpine swift colony at Solothurn occurs in the year 1830. The maximum number of pairs in any one season since careful records have been taken is 229. Many of the birds have been ringed and are now old friends. By ringing, Herr Arn-Willi proved that in one pair the male returned for eighteen seasons and the female for ten—showing that the alpine swift is potentially a long-lived bird. One, taken by air to Nairobi in Kenya by Professor Geigy, of Basle, and released there, was later found at its nest in Solothurn.

On the day of our vigil in the tower the swifts were later than usual in returning: Herr Arn-Willi explained that this was due to the poor weather and consequent scarcity of insect life. A bird with the wing power of the alpine swift, which some authorities consider to be the fastest bird that flies, ranges far for food, and Herr Arn-Willi believes that when the weather in Solothurn is wet, but it is fine in the district of the Alps, his swifts fly there to feed and gather food for their young. As the birds one by one came in from their hunting the church tower was filled with their musical high-pitched trilling cries.

When we left the old church and looked back at the tower, we saw late-comers still flying into the small holes. Their flight was more effortless than the flight of the common swift, and reminded us of shearwaters gliding in at evening to their nesting island from the Atlantic.

In some mountainous valleys of Switzerland alpine swifts are said to share a cliff with colonies of crag martins, but it is worth recording that in Switzerland the alpine swift is less of an alpine bird than the common swift. At Saas-Fee, Zermatt and other townships standing between 5,500 and 6,000 feet above sea level it is common swifts that are seen dashing madly in small parties above the village streets, or circling the tower of the local church, and it is my experience that alpine swifts are only very occasionally present. This may be explained by the fact that Switzerland is near the northern limit of this bird's breeding range in Europe, and that it is less fitted to cope with the frequent changes in weather in the upland districts.

When we arrived at Saas-Fee on 26th June the snow was drifting heavily on the Alps and the temperature was that of a March day. Although the sun shone brightly not a swift was to be seen. The next morning the temperature suddenly rose to summer level and common swifts were everywhere. They must have been held immobile by the complete lack of insect life, and by the cold. Subsequently we saw more than once on fine warm days parties of common swifts 8,500 to 9,000 feet above sea level, and at times pairs visited Riffelalp, 7,300 feet, where we stayed. But we saw no alpine swifts at this height.

Most of the birds of the mountains above the tree-line of the Alps are beautiful. The rock thrush, snowfinch, wall creeper, are exciting and charming. The Alpine accentor, although less brightly plumaged, is an attractive bird. All these from time to time are seen in Britain.

One July afternoon we heard a strange bird on stony ground near a small tarn more than 7,000 feet above sea level. It was tracked and watched, and was a male rock thrush. It was tame, and sat for half an hour, in bright, warm sunshine on a large flat boulder. While resting the bird squatted on its tarsus like a fulmar. After this prolonged rest it hopped sedately, picking up caterpillars and other insects. The head, neck and mantle of this handsome bird were blue, the under parts orange, and the short tail red. Its behaviour was midway between that of a song-thrush and a wheatear. Of its mate there was no sign, and as it did not gather food we imagined that its mate was sitting on a clutch of eggs.

Next day we reached the bird's mountain fastness after nine in the morning. Mist was eddying over the snowy dome of the Bietschhorn, rising to over 14,000 feet, but on our side of the valley the sun shone warmly. We passed, at the edge of a natural forest of larch, banks of *Campanula*; some of the flower-heads were white and dew shone on the hairs of the bells. The bird watcher is thankful that in Switzerland he is not annoyed by midges or mosquitoes on hill ground, but there were a few outsized gadflies, both green and brown-eyed, ready to attack us when we sat. For an hour we waited; at first there was no sign of our friend the rock thrush. Then at last it was seen, some 200 feet above us, on a steep hillside, moving about as it fed. Once it rose almost perpendicularly into the air and soared on motionless wings in song, not planing like a tree pipit but keeping its aerial height as it disappeared over a ridge.

When after a climb of 400 feet we arrived at the ridge, a family of young rock thrushes, strong on the wing, flew out from where they had been sheltering under rocks from the sun. A passing Alpine chough stooped at one bird perched in a small spruce, driving it away. The father of the family had flown down the hill slope at great speed and disappeared. A little later we watched it gathering food for the family and noticed that each time it flew, even for a few yards, it spread wide its bright chestnut tail. The home of the rock thrust was wild and grand. On the far side of the valley glaciers were cracking; high above the main glacier golden eagles soared.

Beside a strong spring many plants of *Saxifraga aizoides* and *Saxifraga stellaris* (both, incidentally, British saxifrages) were in flower. We returned to the floor of the valley through a cluster of summer shielings; the smoke of wood fires was twisting from the holes in their roofs, and in the distance the sound of the bells of cattle mingled with an Alpine ring ousel's song.

Through most of the high valleys of Switzerland swift glacier rivers flow, turgid with silt blown on to the glacier perhaps thousands of years before. In a deep river gorge, where larch and mountain pine grow, a pair of wall creepers were nesting behind a thundering waterfall. The wall creeper is, in flight, a strange and almost fantastic bird. The wings are short, and are broad to the tips—like a miniature golden eagle's wings except that there are no upturned primaries. The progress is wandering like that of a butterfly; indeed, the French name for this bird is 'butterfly of the rocks'. The plumage of the male wall creeper is almost tropical in its brilliance. Its wing coverts are crimson, and the upper parts of the body light grey; the bill is long and curved. The plumage of the female is scarcely less beautiful and unusual. All one morning the creepers unceasingly sought food for their young. They visited grassy banks and rock faces, and eagerly ran up a crack in the rock, often opening with a sudden flick their striking red wings to help their progress. Where a small landslide had brought down some trees and exposed the rock was a favourite hunting ground.

In the late afternoon a male rock bunting came and sang on a branch of the small dead larch beneath which we sat. Its song resembled that of a reed bunting. Later, it flew across the gorge, but returned to the larch. Its grey throat, black-striped head, and its reddish-brown underparts made it an eye-catching bird. The next morning, the heat-wave continuing, we saw house-martins for the first time hawk insects above the gorge, coming up from the valley far below. It was most unexpected for a pair to alight on a branch of the larch, perching close together side by side and remaining for some minutes.

A carrion crow from time to time flew furtively over the gorge and the shrill whistle of a marmot was heard. Marmots haunted the hillside where, a little later, we watched an Alpine accentor (it and the snowfinch and, of course, the ubiquitous Alpine chough are the only birds to be found above 10,000 feet) gathering material for its nest. This bird is inconspicuous on the wing, but when observed more closely its chestnut-streaked flanks give it a touch of distinction. It frequents rocky ground and nests usually in holes in cliffs. At about seven o'clock in the evening, after a day of intense heat, we were walking beneath a rocky face when, only a few yards ahead of us on the track, we came upon an Alpine accentor gathering grass stems. It was remarkably tame and continued working as though we did not exist.

The snowfinch, a bird of the high Alpine country, has surprisingly (for it is a strong flier) several times been blown across to the south-east coast of England. At rest it is not impressive, but on taking flight its snow-white wings at once transform it to a thing of beauty. Although it is a shy and rather nervous bird it is found nesting in mountain huts and hotels. One of the highest hotels in Switzerland is that standing at the summit of the Gornergrat, 10,300 feet above the sea. Here at least two pairs of snowfinches habitually nest. This year the snow lay deep there even in mid-summer.

We came to it beneath a cloudless sky, and the snowy landscape was brilliant. There was a quick flash of white as a snowfinch emerged from high up on the hotel, circled a moment, then flew with swift and powerful flight down the steep hill to search for food for its family on the snow-free ground lower down. At 7,300 feet is a building once used as a hotel laundry. It is now derelict and is used by a pair of snowfinches and a pair of black redstarts as a nesting place. The cock black redstart was an idle fellow and took little part in gathering food for the brood. Both snowfinches worked very hard for their family. The nesting site was at the edge of the forest of larch and Arolla pine, and the birds always flew out of sight uphill towards a marmot-haunted corrie to gather food. Sometimes there was a flutter of snowy wings as both birds returned with food at the same time. Citril finches and serins habitually fed and drank near, and a redpoll used to sing on the roof. It was delightful to watch this bird colony with the majestic Matterhorn and the no less spectacular Weisshorn as a background.

No essay on birds of the Alps would be complete without mention of the Alpine chough. The bill of the common chough is red; the bill of the Alpine bird is parchment-coloured. They are beautiful soarers, and when seen close the upturned wing primaries and the opening and shutting of the tail like a fan can be seen. These characteristics also mark the soaring of the golden eagle. The choughs have been seen on the summit of the Matterhorn, which is almost 15,000 feet high—flying there to share the climbers' morning meal.

An Historic Cairn in Argyll

In the Highlands of Argyll, between Loch Awe and the Firth of Lorne, is a wide area of moor, bog and loch, the home of hill fox, raven and eagle; of hardy sheep and cattle, and a few red grouse. A map of this area shows many place-names, all in Gaelic, of the hills and glens, freshwater lochs, and burns. It is sad to think that the Gaelic language has almost gone from here, and that few of the present generation know the meaning of these names, or indeed how to pronounce them.

One map name (it is written with capital letters) which may attract attention is CARN CHAILEIN; this, translated into English, is Cairn of Colin. Readers familiar with the Gaelic titles of Gaelic chiefs will know that the Celtic title of the chief of Clan Campbell is Mac Chailein, Son of Colin, and that he, the Duke of Argyll, takes this hereditary title from his distinguished ancestor Cailein Mór, Great Colin, whose burial place is at Kilchrenan, near the shore of Loch Awe. This great freshwater loch, the home of salmon, trout and the huge *Salmo ferox*, is four miles distant from another loch of considerable size, Loch Avich. From the west end of Loch Avich a rough road winds among hills and lochs to Loch Scammadal and Glen Euchar. Near its crest this track passes close to the Fiddlers' Well, ice-cold even in summer, and the walker sees below him Loch na Sreinge with its small island. Rather less than a mile north of this loch, on the side of this rough primitive road, is a very old moss-grown cairn of considerable size, marking the spot where Cailein Mór, Great Colin, chief of his clan, was slain in a fierce fight with the MacDougalls about the year 1293.

At that time the MacDougalls were even more powerful than the Campbells. They were descended from Dugal, eldest son of Somerled, Lord of the Isles, and as Lords of Lorne were perhaps the most powerful family in the west. At the time of the battle this cairn commemorates, the Campbells and the MacDougalls were at variance over the boundary between their respective territories. The two chiefs agreed to meet at Loch na Sreinge and discuss these boundaries at the small burn which falls into the loch and which is still known as the Burn of the Conference. Those were the days when might was right, and both chiefs were prudent enough to have a considerable force of clansmen with them, armed with bow-and-arrow and claymore. The MacDougall chief, and his men, came from the west, and rested at Loch Scammadal. Here the clan's magic crystal was produced which, in the hands of a seer during certain rites, foretells the outcome of a fateful meeting. The crystal, to the dismay of those present, fell from the hands of the seer, struck a rock on the shore of the loch, and when picked up was found to be cracked. It is said that because of this dark omen MacDougall of Rara, senior cadet of the clan, then returned home with his men, but the chief with his followers continued, heavy-hearted, on their journey to the pre-arranged meeting ground at Loch na Sreinge.

Much time had been lost because of the disaster to the crystal, and the Campbells, thinking that the MacDougalls no longer wished to assert their claim, began to advance into MacDougall territory. It is not surprising, therefore, that the MacDougalls, seeing their land being invaded by the Campbells, dismissed any thought of a conference, and a desperate battle began. The MacDougalls, now that MacDougall of Rara and his men had turned back, were inferior in numbers, and it seemed as though they would be defeated when one of their archers, sheltered by a boulder high on the opposite side of the glen, fired his arrow from the great distance of around 1,500 yards, and, so sure was his aim, inflicted a mortal wound on Cailein Mór. The name of that archer is no longer known, but the boulder that concealed him is still pointed out. The sorely pressed MacDougalls now attacked with great spirit and courage and the Campbells withdrew, carrying with them the body of their chief, Cailein Mór. So great was the slaughter in this clan fight that the burn where the combat was fiercest ran red with blood. The ford across the stream to this day bears the name Allt Dearg, Red Burn, commemorating the blood of the slain.

The day on which I visited this historic cairn was dark, and in keeping with the grim traditions of the place. Ravens with deep, far-carrying croaking passed overhead swiftly, and I remembered that this bird has special associations with the MacDougalls and that their war banner was in the form of a raven. There are, even at the present day, few visitors who pass along this hill track, and fewer still who know the history of this large heap of stones, which has weathered the winter storms of nearly 700 years.

The cracked crystal is still in the keeping of the chief of the MacDougalls; the crack in it, which was received on the day of that fight long ago, brings vividly to the mind days when a Highland chief and his clan held their land by the power of the sword.

Summer on the High Cairngorms

On a brilliant morning of late July I looked across the foothills of Rothiemurchus Forest to the Cairngorm range. Only the week before, there had been drifting snow on Ben MacDhui, but now full summer had suddenly arrived, and the air was of that extreme clearness associated with Strathspey and Upper Deeside.

The flower buds of the ling were already pink, and the air was fragrant with the scent of Scots firs. One tree that I passed was of mighty girth and was in vigorous growth, although its age may well have been three centuries or even more. Another, equally old, had long since died, and its companion, a birch of like age, was also lifeless. The limbs of both these great trees had been bleached by summer sun and winter frost, like the fir a few miles to the west, which had been chosen by a pair of ospreys for their eyrie this year. In the long heather a greyhen's almost full-grown brood showed little fear. Redstarts flew through the forest clearing above which, earlier in the season, a greenshank had sung his wild and stirring song.

With August near, it was unusual to see winter snowfields of great size still lying in the north corries of the high Cairngorms. The powdery snow of the past winter had drifted into great wreaths; in April an experienced observer estimated that one of those drifts was more than 100 feet in depth.

Many more people now visit the Eastern Cairngorms. A good road has been made from Loch Morlich to the shoulder of Cairngorm (4,084 feet)—the hill that has given its name to the range that in old days was known as Monadh Ruadh, the Red Hill Range, from the colour of some of the slopes. This new road allows motorists to drive to a height of rather more than 2,000 feet. Thence, in 6½ minutes, one is transported by chair-lift to within 300 feet of the summit of Cairngorm. It is a curious sensation to feel the air temperature swiftly drop during the ascent, and to be deposited on a plateau high above the heather line, where the Arctic willow (*Salix herbacea*) takes its place and the ptarmigan croaks. I was told that a ptarmigan had nested within three feet of where men were at work erecting a snow fence. Despite much hammering and human activity, the brooding bird sat tight and hatched her chicks.

When the approach road and the chairlift were visualized, many people feared that much of the charm of the Forest of Glenmore and Cairngorm itself would be destroyed, but the road is already harmonizing with the scenery, and the chair-lift enables thousands of skiers to enjoy their pastime on the high slopes from late autumn until the following summer. On my visit last year in early July men and women were still skiing on large snowfields: this year, in late July, the snow was less accessible.

On the hill of Cairngorm there are two celebrated snowfields. One is in a hollow named Ciste Meararad, Margaret's Chest, and usually remains unmelted throughout the summer. I used to hear a tradition in Rothiemurchus that the Meararad or Margaret it commemorated herded cattle that had their summer pasture on the Cairngorm summit plateaux, and that in her spare time she searched for Cairngorm crystals, having her 'chest' or hiding-place for these precious stones in the hollow that commemorates her. It is curious that another snowbed that lies until late summer on Carn Bàn Mór in Glen Feshie Forest bears the same name.

Between Ciste Meararad and the top of Cairngorm is a historic spring, the Marquess's Well, at approximately 4,000 feet above sea level. Tradition narrates that the name commemorates the Marquess of Huntly, who pursued MacCailein, Marquess of Argyle, westward after the Battle of Glenlivet in 1590.

Near the head of Coire Cas, a north-facing corrie of Cairngorm, is a great snowbed that is a summer landmark from distant hills, such as Morven in Caithness. It is one of the few snowfields in Scotland that carry a name and is called Cuithe Crom, the Bent Snow Wreath, because it is in the form of a sickle. This great snow-bed survived the heat-wave of early June, and still loomed vast at the edge of the clouds on the day when a friend and I saw it six weeks later.

The chair-lift on Cairngorm gives a Continental atmosphere to the place: it did not, therefore, seem surprising to see a reindeer being fed on sandwiches by tourists. I pictured to myself the outraged amazement with which the old deerstalkers of a past generation would have witnessed the scene. The chair-lift, too, has altered the bird life of Cairngorm. In summer the black-headed gulls that nest in colonies on Strathspey have found that the discarded remains of many lunches and teas eaten by visitors provide an easy food supply. At the car-park the gulls stand in rows, or fly overhead. We saw them later performing aerobatics high above the summit of Cairngorm.

The gulls, indeed, act in the same manner as the Alpine choughs on the airy cone of the Matterhorn. The choughs share the climbers' lunch and then, with high-pitched voices, become airborne and slant swiftly high above the vast glaciers to the Gornergrat. There, 10,200 feet above sea level, the mountain railway has its terminus and the white-winged snowfinch nests high on the hotel. The Cairngorms are less than a third of the height of the Alps, yet on their upper slopes and plateaux are to be found some of the plants that grow on the Swiss mountains. This year, as last, these small prostrate plants were late in flowering.

Even in late July it was possible to find *Silene acaulis*, the cushion pink, still in bud, and I have now had the unusual experience of finding it in flower in three consecutive months. At the beginning of May, when the Cairngorms were still under deep snow, there were cushions in full blossom near the sea in the north wing of the Isle of Skye; a month later it added a touch of colour on Beinn Storr on the same island; and now, late in July, the rosy flowers, some spoilt by unusual July snowfalls, were attracting the hardy black Alpine moths to sip their honey high above the valley of the Spey. It was even more unusual to find the pink china-like flowers of the Alpine azalea (*Loiseleuria procumbens*) on the gravelly ridges, as in a warm season it is in flower early in June.

On the south slopes one is dependent upon one's unaided efforts to climb to the high Cairngorms. A few days after reaching Cairngorm by way of its chair-lift we made our way on foot from Derry Lodge in Mar Forest (the shooting-lodge is built 1,400 feet above the sea), up Glen Luibeg to the high, wind-swept slopes of Ben MacDhui (4,300 feet), by way of the Sron Riach approach. In the glen each Scots fir seedling has in the past been devoured by red deer. For the past fifty years I have done my best to persuade the 'powers that be' to fence in small areas here and there, to permit the young trees to spring up. This, I am glad to say, has at length been done since my last visit three years ago, and it is pleasant to see vigorous young seedlings appearing through the heather. An effort is also being made to bring back the Scots fir by fencing and reseeding an area in lonely Glen Guisachan some seven miles to the west. As its Gaelic name implies, Glen Guisachan is Glen of the Fir Wood, but it is now treeless, and has been so for generations.

We passed the Tree of Gold and the Robbers' Thicket; and, as we climbed beyond the glen and reached higher ground, we encountered driving rain and squalls of gale-force wind. On the exposed slope of Sron Riach, at a height of approximately 3,200 feet above the sea, we passed the Scots fir that may be the highest above sea level in Scotland. The tree grows in bush form, for it has been cropped repeatedly by red deer, but it remains vigorous, with many young shoots.

No Night on Iona

There is no night in June on the small Hebridean island of Iona. In Gaelic the name of this island is I, or Hi. Professor W. J. Watson in his valuable work, *History of the Celtic Place-names of Scotland*, gives it as his opinion that this curious name of I or Hi means the Yew-isle. He writes:

> The island may well have been the seat of a yew-culture of which we may possibly have a trace in the legend of Fer Hi, the foster son of Manannan, whose home was in the Western Isles. It is relevant to note the tradition in the Irish *Life of Columba*, that Columba found Druids before him in Hi and expelled them.

As is well known, the Yew played an important part in Druidic rites. The days of the Druids ended on Iona with the arrival of Saint Columba and his twelve followers in the year 563.

On Hi, or Iona as it is now usually named, sunset and afterglow in mid-summer merge at midnight as the track of the invisible sun (on the longest day sunset on Iona is at 10.25 p.m.) moves from north-west to north, and then to north-east. It was eleven o'clock in the evening when I stood at the north shore of Iona and looked across the green machair and white sands to the distant peaks of the Cuillin of Rum rising dark against the afterglow fifty miles to the north. Darker still was the more distant hill range of the Cuillin of Skye. The Skye peaks brought to my mind the expedition of Saint Columba to Skye where he baptized a Pictish chief named Artbrannan, an old man who died after baptism. He was buried where he was baptized, and a cairn was raised over his grave. Adamnan, ninth abbot of Hi, writing a century after Saint Columba's death, tells us that the cairn may still be seen on the coast of Skye, and that the river in which he was baptized was known as Dobur Artbrannan. Though it has intrigued Celtic scholars, the whereabouts of this place-name has never been discovered.

Iona is less than a mile from the Island of Mull. On a June night the ocean strait, amethystine in the twilight, seems much broader, and Mull is remote and mysterious. Throughout the night, except for a brief interval, the corncrake called. It was pleasant to find it still on Iona for this bird has disappeared from most Scottish districts and almost its last stronghold is on Hebridean islands. In the Hebrides both cuckoo and corncrake are said to be 'working' when they are calling. 'The corncrake is working to-day' is a common expression, for the voice of both these birds tells that summer is near. The only trees on Iona are in the garden of the manse. Here is a small rookery, and when I was on the island the rooks were being smitten with a deadly illness; dead and dying birds were being picked up daily. It was unexpected to hear, mingled with the harsh calls of the rooks, the urgent, excited cooing of collared doves. These birds, unknown in Britain thirty years ago, are immigrants from south-east Europe. They first appeared on the east coast of England and have now spread to Mull, Iona and Skye, and even to South Uist and Lewis of the Outer Hebrides. Unless, like the early Celtic saints, they survive a 700-mile sea flight to Iceland, their migration towards the north-west must end on the Outer Hebrides.

In summer the manse garden on Iona is the home of many birds. Fuchsia bushes as high as trees are in flower before the end of May and a short time before my visit a golden oriole on its migration stayed for a time here. The garden, protected by higher ground to the south-west, is comparatively sheltered when Atlantic storms of great violence rush across the island. During a hurricane a crofter's hens were blown with such violence against a wire fence that they were killed.

The sun was warm on the machair of Iona as a companion and I crossed to the west shore. Here is a large green knoll named Sithein Mór; it is traditionally said to be the Angels' Knoll, where Columba once communed with angels. Near it is the shore where the saint prophesied that a crane (a bird that at the time nested in Great Britain and Ireland) would arrive on Iona. In *The Life of Saint Columba*, Book I, is the following account of the occurrence:

> While the saint was living on Iona he called one of the brothers and thus addressed him: 'In the morning of the third day from this date thou must sit down and wait on the shore on the western side of this island, for a Crane, which is a stranger from the northern region of Hibernia and hath been driven about by various winds, shall come, weary and fatigued, after the ninth hour, and lie down before thee on the beach quite exhausted. Treat that bird tenderly, take it to some neighbouring house, where it may be kindly received and carefully nursed and fed by thee for three days and three nights. When the Crane is refreshed

with the three days' rest, and is unwilling to abide any longer with us, it shall fly back with renewed strength to the pleasant part of Ireland from which it originally hath come. This bird do I consign to thee with such special care because it cometh from our own native place.' The brother obeyed, and on the third day, after the ninth hour, he watched as he was bid for the arrival for the expected guest. As soon as the Crane came and alighted on the shore, he took it up gently in its weakness and carried it to a dwelling that was near, where in its hunger he fed it. On his return to the monastery in the evening, the saint, without any enquiry, but as stating a fact, said to him, 'God bless thee, my child for thy kind attention to this foreign visitor, that shall not remain long on its journey, but return within three days to its old home.' As the saint predicted, so exactly did the event prove, for after being nursed carefully for three days, the bird then gently rose on its wings to a great height in the sight of its hospitable entertainer, and marking for a little its path homewards, it directed its course across the sea to Hibernia straight as it could fly, on a calm day.

It will be noticed that the crane had come from, and was returning to, the land of the saint's birth. It is many centuries since the crane nested in Ireland. The west shore of Iona can have changed little since Columba's day. Dun I, highest hill of the island, rises in grassy terraces here. They were bright with the blue flowers of *Scilla verna*, the spring squill, on the early June morning when we climbed this hill, which commemorates in its name the old name of Iona. On islets a little way out to sea, oystercatchers were sun-bathing and on some of the wee islands sea thrift spread a red carpet to high tide-mark. Swallows were flying across the hill and ravens patrolled the shore. There are fewer lapwings than formerly on Iona, and the *twite* (or mountain linnet) also is less numerous.

Mist dropped on Ben Mor Mull and the mutter of distant thunder was heard, but on Iona the sun continued to shine. The flood tide began to flow through the Sound of Iona and I thought of stormy days fifty years ago when Coll Maclean the ferryman sailed his small undecked boat, well reefed, across the crested seas, while his passengers lay on the bottom of the boat to give him an unrestricted view of breaking waves on his course.

The following morning as we crossed the strait in an open motor boat ocean mist half hid Dun I, and I remembered the old tradition that, even before Columba's time, the Druids could conjure up a magic mist, or even a magic sea on dry land. Manannan the sea god (the Isle of Man bears his name) could become invisible by throwing a magic cloak across his shoulders, and a mound on Iona has the name Dun Manannan, Manannan's Fort. Blue sunlit sea, blue sky and a white mist half-concealing Columba's Island cheered us as we steered east to the Ross of Mull.

Castle at the Gateway to Skye

At daybreak across the quiet waters of Loch Duich the snowy peaks of the Sisters of Kintail rose cold and stern at the head of the loch. On a low, rocky promontory a heron stood as though carved in stone. The ground rises steeply from the south shore of the loch and it is February before the sun shines on the houses of the small township of Letterfearn.

Beyond the sheltered house of Druideig old trees grow to the edge of the tide. One of these ancient trees is an oak with an interesting history. Up to about 100 years ago sailing ships of considerable size were built at Dornie, on the opposite side of the sea loch. It was considered that this oak, because of its shape, would be specially valuable in fashioning the keel of a new vessel to be built. The sum of £1 was, therefore, offered to the proprietor of the ground but was refused. That was 100 years and more ago, and the oak must, therefore, be of great age. It is still alive, and has indeed the appearance of a very old tree, although there are many larger and more distinguished trees in the wood. The ship for which this tree was intended was the *Donnan Castle*, a three-masted schooner of 300 tons, which later traded with Baltic and north European ports. She was ultimately in collision with another ship off Lizard Point and sank, far from her home sea loch. There are lichens on the branches of this old oak, which might well have ended its days a century ago, and roe deer crop the grass in the open parts of the wood.

A few hundred yards farther along the shore of the loch the road ends at Totaig, where there was formerly a public ferry across to Dornie. Here a shag was drying his wings on a skerry, and a strong tidal river was entering Loch Duich.

The road abruptly ends, but the path, rising gradually, leads along the shore to the remains of a splendid *broch* or *dun* with the curious name Caisteal Gnùgaig. This *broch* is built close to a hill burn which would have provided its occupants with water. An old larch grows beside it and in the greyness of a winter morning the Castle of Eilean Donnan across the strait could be seen. Could the stones of this castle speak, they might tell of centuries of clan warfare and of dark deeds.

It is said that many centuries ago the son of a Kintail chief received his first drink from the skull of a raven. Both the Celts and the Norse believed that the raven was a bird with occult powers, and this drinking rite enabled the infant to understand the language of birds. When he came to manhood he travelled to France. The King of France could get no sleep because of the music of the birds in the grounds of the royal residence. The young Highlander who could speak to birds in their own language, was asked if he could help. He held a conference with the birds and they obligingly agreed to make music beyond earshot of those in the palace. As a mark of his gratitude the King of France made him a present of a fully manned ship. In this vessel he journeyed to many lands, and at last returned to his sea loch. He was now wealthy and respected, and Alexander II, King of Scotland at this time, commissioned him to build the Castle of Eilean Donnan as a defence against raiding Norsemen.

The Castle of Eilean Donnan has withstood many sieges. In the year 1590 Donald Gorm MacDonald, chief of his clan, sailed with his war galleys across the strait from Skye hoping to take the castle, which was then lightly garrisoned. The defenders were said to have numbered no more than three, and when their resistance had apparently ended Donald Gorm, showing himself rashly, was hit in the leg by an arrow. In his anger he tore out the arrow roughly by the shaft, almost severing an artery. He was carried to his war galley and taken to a low grassy isle, named Glas Eilean, rising at a little distance from the castle. Here, in a rough shelter that was hastily built for him, his followers attempted to stop the bleeding of the wound, but in vain.

The place where he died is still named Larach Tigh Mhic Dhomhnall, which can be translated 'Site of MacDonald's House'. We know that the Castle of Eilean Donnan was a fortress at the time of the first Jacobite rising in 1715, and at the Battle of Glenshiel in 1719 a force of Spaniards assisted at an abortive Jacobite rising, having been brought by sea and quartered in the Castle of Eilean Donnan. They were defeated by government forces, and later the castle was heavily bombarded by government war vessels. For nearly two centuries it remained a ruin, but was restored by Colonel MacRae-Gilstrap, whose ancestors were the constables of the castle.

In the dim winter I looked across the strait to the misty Cuillin of Skye and saw the Outer Island mail steamer approach the pier at Kyle of Lochalsh. The high moor where I stood was in its winter sleep and thus, near a clear spring, it was exciting to come upon a large colony of the yellow saxifrage (*Saxifraga aizoides*). This plant has a much longer period of flowering than any other Highland saxifrage. The seed-heads were still full of unshed seeds, and the leaves of the plants were green and vigorous, and ready for the sunshine of spring to stimulate their growth in the coming summer.

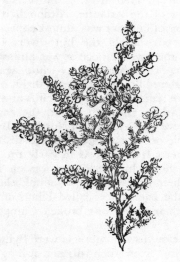

In the Haunts of the Chough

The sun was warm on the Hebridean island of Islay and shone on the clear green water of the Atlantic. Although it was as late as mid-summer, the song of curlews was almost continuous above the moors, where small colonies of the butterwort held deep blue flower-heads to the blue sky. The ocean was almost at rest, but at intervals a wandering wave broke snow-white against dark cliffs almost hidden by clustered flowers of the sea thrift, in which herring gulls were nesting. We reached the highest cliffs and saw, across the sea, the Island of Rathlin and, beyond it, the coast and hills of Northern Ireland. Between Rathlin and Northern Ireland flows one of the most formidable ocean currents in the British Isles. Rathlin, now a part of Northern Ireland, was in early times ruled by the Lords of the Isles whose chief residence was on Islay, and who were crowned, on their accession, on a small island of an Islay loch. The Lords of the Isles, often called Kings of the Isles, were MacDonalds; when their power was broken Campbells succeeded them.

Six hundred feet below us five gannets were flying, low over the Atlantic, in single line from their distant fishing grounds, and steering a steady course for their great nesting colony on Ailsa Craig below the south-east horizon. No one has explained, or perhaps knows, why gannets on these long journeys fly almost always in odd numbers; this can be verified by any observer who counts the birds as they pass through some narrow channel such as the Sound of Harris.

We sat in sunshine in a small grassy corrie full-open to the sun and sheltered from the north-west wind. A raven sailed slowly and with dignity along the cliff's edge, and suddenly we saw a dramatic attack made on it by an oystercatcher which had young far beneath us at the cliff foot. An oystercatcher rarely soars, but this particular bird showed surprising powers of flight. On a wind current it quickly rose, calling excitedly, to the cliff top. When the raven noticed its assailant it rose much higher and thought no doubt that it had shaken it off; but in a few seconds the oyster-catcher had soared above it. The raven seemed surprised, but when they had passed beyond our sight the oystercatcher was continuing to press home its attacks, with shrill, angry whistling.

We waited long for the appearance of choughs, and it seemed as though we should be disappointed, when, in a second of time, they were there. A pair, flying in from the moor behind the cliff, appeared suddenly over the edge of the corrie. They had not noticed us, and in gay and joyous flight, their glossy blue-black plumage shining in the sun, they dipped, and passed close together, low over the floor of the corrie. As they came abreast of us, one of the pair uttered a high musical whistle as if in greeting. Then, more quickly than it takes to narrate, the birds were gone; but that sudden vision of beauty and grace will remain in our memories.

We remained sitting quietly, and half an hour later again saw one of the birds. It was busily turning over sheep droppings, eagerly searching for worms and beetles below them; its bill was deep red in the sunlight. Later that day a second pair of choughs followed the same line of flight through the corrie. This, or another pair, we subsequently watched on the moor probing the ground with their strong bills.

The fine weather continued and the mid-summer migration of swallows, but not of swifts, continued, when, two days later, we again climbed to the moorland and high cliffs of the chough. On this day heated air rising from the sun-warmed rocks enabled the choughs to display their soaring powers. One pair flying across the moor met the buoyancy of a thermal when almost over us and began to rise. On their broad wings, with primary feathers widely spaced, eagle-fashion, the two birds, light and buoyant as the proverbial feather, rose higher and higher. It is said that the peregrine falcons that were nesting farther along the coast make raids on the chough population, but the chough is better able to take care of itself than the two carrier pigeons which were lying side by side on a grassy ledge above the peregrine's eyrie.

That evening the full song of curlews, some near, others more distant, never ceased although the sun was hot and the moor dry and almost parched. It is curious that on Skye the curlew is uncommon as a nesting species and on Islay, in similar surroundings, there is a large nesting population. On Islay also there is a far larger population of lapwings.

Tales of Monsters in Highland Lochs

The Loch Ness Monster has attracted so much publicity that little attention has been paid to other Highland lochs which traditionally are the home of a creature of similar habits and appearance. Loch Morar, the deepest freshwater loch in Scotland—its depth exceeds 1,000 feet—has in its depths a creature which has been reported to me on more than one occasion. The name of this creature is Mhorag; it is usually reported as having three humps. Its appearance was, in a less sophisticated age, believed to portend the death of a MacDonald of Morar, or of a Gillies.

I heard from the owner of a motor boat of the sudden appearance of the Beast of Loch Morar. The boat's owner was taking a party of visitors in his launch to the head of this long, dark loch, where I have seen a golden eagle sail like a gigantic shearwater across the path of a boat and where high hills rise steeply to the clouds. All at once a huge creature emerged, with much splashing and the throwing of spray, only a few yards from the boat.

The boat owner told me that, had he been alone, his story would not have been believed, but all his passengers saw it and thus put it on record that a creature far larger than a seal had surfaced on Loch Morar. Long before there was a motor boat on Loch Morar the people of the district from time to time saw what seemed to be a boat towing two or three smaller boats at speed up the loch. It was supposed that this was the Mhorag, and that the small boats on tow were in reality its humps showing above the water.

The Loch Ness Monster is more frequently reported than the Beast of Loch Morar, but this is only natural, as Loch Morar lies in a remote and sparsely populated area, with no main road along its shore.

Loch Shiel in the West Highlands also has its Beast, named Seilag by the local people. I have heard of no recent appearance of the Seilag, but here again no road runs by the shore of this long and deep freshwater loch.

The theory that these creatures are landlocked sea animals is supported by the fact that Loch Ness, Loch Morar, and Loch Shiel are all so near sea level that they must at one time have been tidal lochs. Indeed it would seem possible that sea water may even now remain in their depths. A team of scientists from the Institute of Oceanography at the University of British Columbia in Canada has carried out observations in Powell Lake, some eighty miles north of Vancouver. This freshwater lake was once an inlet of the sea. The area of salt water begins at a depth below the surface of approximately 400 feet. The concentration of salt increases with depth; the salinity of the water at the bottom of the lake is half that of the sea water in the Strait of Georgia less than a mile away.

The scientists who made these observations think that the sea water now deep in Powell Lake was trapped somewhere between 7,300 and 12,250 years ago. It is not without interest that the depth of Powell Lake, namely 1,180 feet, is almost exactly the same as the deepest part of Loch Morar. The research work in Powell Lake was a result of reports by a Norwegian oceanographer, who found salt water at the bottom of two Norwegian lakes.

This scientific research raises the question: is there perhaps a deep-seated layer of salt water in one or more of the Scottish freshwater lochs where large, unknown creatures reputedly have their home? Until now, so far as I know, there has been no testing of the deep waters of our home inland lochs for an area of salinity, and it would seem that this opens a fascinating field of future investigation.

Loch Ness certainly has never been known to have ice on it. In the words of an old manuscript, 'The lake never freezeth and if a lump of ice is cast into it, it soon after dissolveth'. The writer goes on to mention the possibility of a subterranean communication between Loch Ness and the sea, and he certainly would have been thrilled by the discoveries in Powell Lake.

Flowers and Birds of Skye

In the summer of 1773 the distinguished traveller and naturalist, Thomas Pennant, visited Skye. Now, nearly two hundred years later, the illustration in his book of that attractive and uncommon plant of the Scottish hills and glens, *Dryas octopetala*, is as lifelike as ever and could scarcely be improved upon by present-day standards. Pennant tells us that a hill in the south of Skye, Ben Suardal by name, 'is in a manner covered with that rare plant *Dryas octopetala*'.

Reading his account, I thought that a visit to the hill fifty-five miles from our home in the north of the island (few persons realize the size of Skye) would be of interest; and accordingly, on a summer day of blue sky, clear air and blue sea, I travelled through Skye, past Uig nestling at the head of its bay, past Portree, capital of the island, past Sligachan beneath the Black Cuillin, where drifts of the past winter's snow still lay on the north-facing gabbro rocks, and as I approached Broadford I saw the slopes of Ben Suardal ahead of me.

In a recent book on mountain flowers a botanist of authority gives his opinion that the hills of Scotland might rival those of Scandinavia in the wealth of the Alpine flora if they were not so heavily grazed by sheep in summer. It is very true. *Dryas octopetala* still covers Ben Suardal, as in Pennant's day, but where are the eight-petalled flowers which delight the nature lover? Sheep, and to a lesser extent rabbits, graze the plants so closely that scarcely a single cream-coloured flower is to be seen. The plants themselves, close-cropped, still carpet the ground.

Most people know the common butterwort, its greenish-yellow leaves growing in boggy ground in the shape of a starfish, but the rarer and smaller *Pinguicula lusitanica*, with flowers of a lighter blue and flowering a month later than the common species, is a scarce and local plant. This too is found in Skye. During the past summer I visited a site where formerly there was no difficulty in finding *P. lusitanica* in flower, but not a blossom was seen. Each flower or seedhead of the larger and more robust *P. vulgaris* had been cropped by sheep, and I have little doubt that this had happened to the smaller species also. The very rare white-flowered *P. alpina*, which was formerly in Skye, has quite disappeared, and indeed may be said to be extinct in the Highlands of Scotland. Is it possible that sheep are responsible?

One of the rarest mountain plants in Scotland, *Diapensia lapponica*, found not far, as the eagle flies, from the Isle of Skye, is heavily grazed by sheep, which pasture over its windswept habitat and crop its delicate creamy-white flowers. That very rare cress, *Arabis alpina*, which is found in Britain only on the Cuillin hills of Skye, is safe from sheep in its rocky habitat.

Skye is the home of a small plant, with a still smaller flower, *Koenigia islandica*, which until a few years ago was not known in Britain. It is found on the hills of Skye, and grows and flowers on the most barren and windswept screes, where it has no plant competition. It is so insignificant and, strange as it may seem, so numerous, that it is safe from collectors. It was formerly thought to be no nearer Skye than Iceland; during the past year it has been found also on the Isle of Mull.

Of birds, Skye holds more than one pair of golden eagles, but the eagles which are often reported to me by visitors, who (as they write or telephone) see them perched on telegraph posts, are almost certainly buzzards. Both buzzard and kestrel have fed on the plague of field voles which increased to extraordinary numbers during 1956 and 1957. Two March blizzards told heavily on the voles, and there are now few to be seen, but as the rabbit is coming back the buzzards at all events will continue to feed well.

It is curious, considering the size and suitability of the island lochs, that no black-throated diver nests here and there are very few pairs of red-throated divers. Nesting dunlin are also extremely scarce. Sea birds are not so numerous as might be expected. The fulmar petrel has at least three colonies in Skye, but there is no large kittiwake colony on the island. The golden plover nests on the moors, but the curlew is a winter visitor rather than a nester, and there are large areas of the island, apparently suitable, where no curlew's call or trilling song is heard. The corncrake is still a regular summer visitor to Skye. One year in May, before the grass was long, a pair of corncrakes courted only a few yards from our window, and in full view as we sat at meals. Sedge warblers have increased, and in June and early July their attractive song is heard at midnight, a full hour before that early singer, the lark, mounts into the sky to greet the sunrise.

Actually, in clear weather at mid-summer in the Isle of Skye there is no darkness, but dusk lies mysteriously between sunset and sunrise.

During those hours the hills of the Outer Hebrides rise black and clear-cut. In exceptionally clear weather Hirta of St Kilda is visible from the hills in the north of Skye and seems to lie far out on a mysterious sea as the sun rises, deep red, glowing and huge, above the hills of Strath Dionard, eighty miles to the north-east.

Scarba and its Whirlpool

The sun set in splendour behind Muile nam Mór Bheann, Mull of the Great Hills, and the young moon, golden and benign, sank very slowly beyond the rocky coast of Jura of the Caves. North of Jura rose the high island of Scarba, still clear-cut but dark as night. The evening breeze awoke, gently shepherding small waves over the silent, sleeping sea and arousing it from its dreams.

The wind of dusk was short-lived; next morning the sky was without a cloud as we sailed across from Craignish on the mainland to Scarba. This is a distinguished but lonely island, its one hill, approximately 1,500 feet in height and haunted by adders, being a landmark from afar. Sir Donald Monro, High Dean of the Isles, wrote of Scarba in the year 1549 as 'an high, roughe yle, inhabit and manurit (cultivated), with some woodes in it'. Little is known of the early inhabitants of Scarba; they have long left it. Mary MacLeod, the celebrated Gaelic poetess whose father was a cousin of the chief of the clan, and who in the course of her long life of 105 years, acted as nurse to five chiefs of the MacLeods was here. As a punishment for a satire she composed on him, the chief banished her for a time to Scarba, where she wrote some of the finest of her songs. When the distinguished traveller Thomas Pennant landed on Scarba in the year 1772 he found forty inhabitants living on the island. His vessel anchored beneath the 'vast mountain of Scarba' which he climbed under the guidance of 'Mr Macleane' who at that time owned the island. Pennant records that the climb was 'through heath of an uncommon height, swarming with grouse'.

Martin Martin, who published his book *A Description of the Western Islands of Scotland* in the year 1703, mentions that only two years before he wrote, a woman 'lived sevenscore years on the Isle of Scarba, and enjoyed the free use of her Senses and Understanding all her days'. The island at the present day (1970) has a population of sheep, red deer and wild goats. There is now only one house, which has not been lived in for some years. At the landing place on the east side of the island we found the sea calm and very clear; jellyfish of various sizes drifted slowly past and there was an unbroken silence over land and sea. The east shore of Scarba is comparatively sheltered and trees grow almost to the tide-mark. We climbed on a rough track, past bracken five feet high, and through a thick wood of deciduous trees of various species. Even in the strong sunlight this wood was dark, except in one place where the clustered berries of a rowan tree were brilliant red. Near the upper margin of this wood it was unexpected to find the remains of an avenue of silver firs, (*Abies nobilis*). They are old trees, still erect and stately, but their tops are lifeless; the salt-laden gales may have been too much for them. High above the deserted house, near which several fallow deer were grazing, a pair of kestrels soared and dived like swifts.

We followed a path which had been made more than half a century ago. It rises gradually to a height of some 800 feet above the sea and after passing near a scattered wood of planted Scots firs leads for several miles round the island. The heather bloom on Scarba is remarkable; in places there was white heather growing close to the path. Through the clear air we looked upon the many hills that formed the horizon east and north-east. The twin, shapely tops of Ben Cruachan (the name in its true Gaelic form is Cruachan Beann which, translated, means Haunch of Peaks) were prominent, and at the head of distant and invisible Loch Etive we saw Beinn Starav, home of the ptarmigan, and Bidein nam Beann, highest hill in Argyll, near it. Across the blue Atlantic northward rose Ben Buie, Creach Bheinn, and Ben Talaidh—hills of the Island of Mull. The sun was warm and the air dry. The silence was broken by a sound now rarely heard in Britain—the song of the grasshopper, a rustling music that is associated in my memory with summer days of long ago. Grasshoppers cannot resist pesticides; it is good to know they have a retreat on Scarba. A less attractive resident on this island is the adder. We did not see one of these serpents, but at the side of the path was lying an adder's thin delicate skin, recently cast.

Scarba is celebrated for its whirlpool, which is near the Scarba shore in the mile-wide strait which separates Scarba from Jura. The whirlpool's name is Coire Bhreacain, or Breacan's Cauldron, named after a prince of Norway whose galley was overwhelmed here. Breacan loved the daughter of a great Highland chief who may have been the Lord of the Isles. The chief told him that he could marry his daughter if he succeeded in anchoring his galley for three nights in the formidable strait. Breacan returned to Norway and a seer of that country told him to take with him three cables, one of hemp, one of wool, and the third made from maidens' tresses. Breacan was handsome and popular and the maidens of Norway were glad to present him with their cherished hair.

Breacan sailed from Norway to the Hebrides. He anchored his galley, held by the three cables, near the whirlpool. The first night the hemp cable parted, on the second night the cable of wool gave way. The third night came and Breacan knew that his life depended on the hair of the maidens of Norway. The seer had warned him that this hair must come only from maidens of spotless reputation. The night was almost past but as the dawn broke one strand of the cable parted. This was the beginning of the end. The galley was never seen again, but Breacan's body was brought ashore by his faithful hound to the sandy bay of Jura, on the south side of the strait. Martin Martin (1703) tells us curtly that Breacan (he spells the name Brekan) is buried in a cave in the north of Jura, 'as appears from the stone Tomb and Altar there'.

One would give much to know more of this cave, but island tradition is now silent as to the whereabouts of Breacan's grave. On the August afternoon of sunshine when we rested above the blue strait in the sun-warmed heather the Atlantic was at rest and the whirlpool slept, yet all the time the air was filled with a volume of deep sound as of a great river as the flood tide passed through the strait. When a westerly gale fights with that tide, the sound of their battle is heard on the mainland of Argyll, sometimes at a distance of twelve miles. A friend of mine arrived in his yacht off the west entrance to the strait one afternoon in early March. A gale from the west was blowing and driving snow almost hid the land on either side of the strait. The skipper (he was also the owner) of the yacht was a daring character; he decided to continue on his course through the gulf of Coire Bhreacain. The gale urged him on; the strength of a spring tide was against him. For a few minutes he was able to see, through the whirling snow-flakes, the rocky coast of Scarba and was amazed to find that although he was steaming at ten knots he remained stationary. He increased speed to eleven knots, his engines running at full throttle, and anxiously watched the shore. After a time he was thankful to see that the yacht was creeping forward, literally foot by foot. The roar of the sea, the flying spindrift, the whirlpool with the noise of pistol shots spouting high into the air only a few hundred yards from the ship, the currents and eddies that seized his vessel and terrifyingly altered its course; all these things made the passage a hair-raising one. A native of Jura who was a master mariner, when he heard the story, listened in silence; at its close he remarked solemnly and emphatically, 'That man should never be alive.' It is said that Fortune favours the brave. After what seemed an age the ship cleared the strait and passed beyond the ten-knot current. Dusk was falling and anchor was dropped in the lee of Jura.

The Rev. Donald Budge, who was minister on Jura for many years, tells us in his valuable book, *Jura*, of the strange disappearance of a cabin-cruiser without trace in the whirlpool of Coire Bhreacain on a mid-summer day in the year 1951. The engine failed; the passengers and skipper took to the small boat, and when last they saw their vessel she was being drawn irresistibly towards the whirlpool; she vanished completely and no trace of her was ever found.

On this August afternoon as the tide ebbed we watched a low, rocky island slowly emerge from the white foam near the centre of that great tidal river. It is said that occasionally at low water in the rutting season stags swim across from Jura to Scarba and rest awhile on this island. There are other isles, near the Jura shore. During the clan fight when the Campbells of Craignish killed all but two of the Macleans of Jura, a Maclean survivor escaped by swimming, in a strong tide, to one of these isles. The path on Scarba, high above the whirlpool, continues westward until the walker sees ahead of him, out on the blue Atlantic, the Garvelloch Islands, sometimes known as the Isles of the Sea. These are a chain of small islands, and on one of them are beehive cells and a stone on which is incised a cross. There is a tradition that this stone marks the grave of Eithne, mother of Saint Columba whose mystic Isle, Iona, can be seen from the high ground of Scarba on a clear day. Scholars believe that Saint Brendan founded his monastery of Ailech here actually before Columba arrived on Iona from Eire.

A light air current kept off the midges, but when we turned for our long walk to the jetty that air current was with us and they were able to attack in numbers. We passed a hill loch where trout were rising and from here saw the white sails of a ketch moving on the tide through the Dorus Mór or Great Door which marks the tide-beset passage to the Crinan Canal. Far below us was the small wood we had passed that morning: when we at last reached it a pair of buzzards showed us that, like the wren who later scolded us, we were regarded as unwelcome visitors to their territory. All that day we saw no red deer; they, like the wild goats which are said to kill the adders with their hooves, were on the rocky Atlantic side of the island.

We had the last of a favourable tide that evening for the passage across to Craignish, and as we reached deep water a pair of fulmars circled the boat, and shags dived in the tidal stream. The hills of

Mull became faint in the evening haze as the piper tuned his Pìob Mhór and played one of the most beautiful of all pipe tunes, 'Lament for Mary MacLeod' as we looked back upon Scarba, where she had lived in temporary banishment three centuries ago.

Eagles Change Over

The male eagle was sunning himself on a heathery hill-face above the eyrie, where his mate was brooding her two rounded eggs. In the deep cup of the eyrie she was invisible to me until she rose and stood, a queenly figure, before she once more settled herself on the eggs. Her mate stood, surveying in the spring sunshine the rabbit-haunted slopes far below him, while all the time, on the skyline above him and just beyond his vision, the ears of a watching rabbit were just visible to me at my observation post. Then the eagle took wing, sailed along the face of the cliff, and began to rise in wide spirals.

At a height of perhaps 5,000 feet above the cliff a fine-weather cumulus cloud was floating almost motionless. The eagle steered his course until he was beneath this cloud, knowing that the thermals of sun-warmed air rising below it would provide him with the means of climbing without effort. Higher and higher he sailed until he appeared to be little larger than a swift. He then entered the dark depths of the cloud and was lost to view.

Five minutes later as I prepared to leave my post I saw the eagle once more. He had dropped earthward in a breathtaking dive and now was sailing along the face of the cliff. He alighted on a ledge, pulled some heather from the ground, and, carrying it in his strong bill, sailed with it to the eyrie, laying his offering carefully on the nest.

His mate rose stiffly from her brooding, threw herself happily over the cliff, and sailed fast against the fresh breeze, which was now fanning the flames of a distant moorland fire. The husband walked carefully to the eggs, lowered himself over them, and began his turn at incubation. Less than five minutes before he had been sailing at a height of at least 5,000, perhaps considerably more. The air temperature at that height would have been little if any above freezing point and the change to the sun-heated pinnacle which held the eyrie must have been sudden and pleasant.

Not far from the eagle's eyrie is a dipper-haunted waterfall. Above the fall, in the sunlit veil of spray that so often hangs here, a large cushion of the purple mountain saxifrage adds beauty and charm to the austere scene. This saxifrage, of all the flowers of the hills, is easily the first to blossom. It is so spartan that it is unhappy on a south-facing slope and prefers a bleak northerly aspect. Despite the continuous low temperature of March this plant, bathed by icy spray, was in full flower in mid-April.

On ice-beset islets off the Spitsbergen coast I have seen this saxifrage in flower in July and in the same month, at 10,000 feet on the Swiss Alps, have admired its large, almost exotic flowers, which each evening were submerged by a glacial stream, at that hour a foaming torrent of melted ice and snow. The most severe frost has no apparent effect on the flowers of the purple saxifrage. One day when I walked beneath the eagles' cliff, icicles several yards high were gleaming in the sunlight near the plants. With a sudden crash several of these icicles, loosened by the sun's heat, fell to break in a thousand splinters. A dark form sailed then from the cliff above my head. She was the brooding eagle, and evidently considered me responsible for this rude disturbance; I hurriedly left the area as she sailed overhead.

The golden eagle is a model husband and insists on taking periodic spells upon the eggs. One afternoon in April when the husband alighted on the eyrie and stood expectantly, his mate showed no inclination to rise. The eagle waited patiently, but at last, walking up to his mate, he gave her a polite but firm nudge with his golden head; she then rose to her feet, spread her broad wings, and sailed away, to leave him with the responsible task of keeping the eggs warm.

Near my watching place the first arrivals of the clan of the wheatears were spider-catching on the sun-warmed boulders, which only a fortnight before had been snow-covered, and a pair of snipe were courting in swift, erratic flight. The sun had shone for a week from an unclouded sky, yet the moor, hill slopes, and grassy corries were browner than in December, for the early spring, in the High-lands of Scotland as elsewhere in Britain, had been Arctic in the intensity of frost and frequent snowfalls. During a sunny spell which followed three days of cold rain I saw an unusual golden eagle incident.

The eagles were perched on the ridge of their cliff when one of them with a sudden movement spread wide its wings and opened its tail, and in that exceptional position stood facing the breeze and the sun while it dried out its saturated plumage. A cormorant and a shag are often seen drying their wings, but so far as I know there has not been any previous record of an eagle behaving in this way.

Last year this pair of golden eagles had an altogether unusual nesting season. To begin with, a new eyrie was built and the eggs laid at least five weeks later than usual. One eaglet was reared, and at the end of July it was still a month short of making its first flight, five weeks behind schedule. Whether its parents grew tired of feeding what they perhaps regarded as an unsatisfying slow-growing child, or whether they became alarmed by much rabbit-shooting beneath their cliff, no food appeared to be brought latterly to the unfortunate eaglet, and one day it lay lifeless in the eyrie.

Chiefs and their Clansmen

In bygone times Bonds, or as they were then called, Bands of Manrent, were fairly common. In recent years, such a bond is rare, but a member of the House of Gordon Association, who lives in New Zealand, now binds himself legally 'in true manrent and loyal service to the Right Honourable the Marquis of Huntly and Gordon, Chief of the whole name and Kin of Gordon, for all the days of my life'.

A photostatic copy of this bond, supplied to me by Captain Charles Gordon, younger, of Pitlurg, who was Honorary Secretary of the recently formed Association, illustrates this article. I was helped in my researches into this old and little known custom by Sir Iain Moncreiffe of that Ilk, and by Dr William Beattie, Librarian of the National Library of Scotland.

In the fifteenth and sixteenth centuries Bands of Manrent were not uncommon. The Errol Papers, which are printed in the Spalding Club Miscellany, Vol. 2, on this subject, are of great value and interest. On page 252 is printed:

'BAND OF MANRENT OF ALEXANDER MACKINTOCHE, THANE OF RATHAMURCUS: XVII JUNE MCCCCLXXII.'

In this Bond the Thane binds himself 'to be ridin man to my Lorde William Eroll of Eroll Lord the Hay and Constable of Scotland for all dayis of my lyffe/AND that I sall gyve my saide Lorde leile and trew consale efter my knavlage quhen he askis me it/AND I salbe with my saide lorde in weir and in peace for all the dayis of my lywe in contrar and againis all leuande man excep myn allegens to my Soueran Lorde and my manrent to my Lorde of Huntly.'

The Band is dated, 'At Perthe the XVII day of June the yer of God a thowsand four hundrath sevynty and tway yeris.' The early spelling of the place-name of Rothiemurchus is of considerable interest.

The Bands of Manrent published in Vol. 2 of the Spalding Club's Miscellany are 41 in number, and date from 1466 to 1612. Most of them are covenants between the Earl of Erroll, Hereditary High Constable of Scotland, and his kinsmen and neighbours. There

are printed besides two curious deeds. In one of them, given by the
Clan Donnachaidh to the ninth Earl of Erroll (whose grandmother
had been a Robertson of Struan), the clan bind themselves to be
faithful to their own chief. The other is the bond whereby the
Provost, Magistrates and Town Council of Edinburgh bound themselves faithfully to the fourth Earl of Erroll in the year 1508, where-
upon he constituted them his deputies in the office of Constabulary.

Under the modern Clan Society system, when people of other
names (but usually having some vague connection) wish to join a
Clan society, Bonds of Manrent are very occasionally given to the
Chief, in order to secure admission to the Society. A bond of this
kind meets an emotional need in the present materialistic age.

There was also seventeenth- and eighteenth-century declarations
of clanship, acknowledging a particular chief. There are examples
of this in the Black Book of Taymouth from the sixteenth century—
for instance, the MacLaren bond. Striking examples of a bond of
this nature are given in the Scots Peerage, Vol. 8.

In the autumn of 1723 several families bearing the names Bowman
and More, and living in Glenmuich and Glenesk, approached the
sixth Earl of Strathmore, affirming that their true surname was
Lyon. These families had left Angus because of some troubles, and
had assumed the names of Bowman and More. They said they were
by blood of the name of Lyon (Lord Strathmore's family name) and
now desired to resume that name.

The Earl acknowledged the kinship, and they accordingly entered into a bond with him as their Chief and protector, and became
bound to answer his call upon all occasions. The Earl for his part
received them into his protection and acknowledged them to be of
his clan and family. The contract is dated 2nd October 1723, at
Aboyne. It was subscribed by twenty-six heads of families taking the
name of Lyon, and with them, be it noted, was one who subscribed,
'A.G. their pyper.'

Eight years later, in the time of James, seventh Earl of Strathmore,
a sept bearing the unusual name of Breassauch, who had their
homes in Glenshee and Glenisla, declared that Breassauch was
only their borrowed name. They, like the Bowmans and Mores,
desired to assume their true name of Lyon, and to acknowledge the
Earl to be their Chief. The Earl admitted their claim, and acknowledged them to be of his kin and blood. The contract dated at
Glamis Castle, 28th July 1731, is subscribed for the Clan by their
leader Patrick Lyon, who is therein designated Captain Patrick
Lyon, younger, of Innerarity.

Why these families were under the necessity to change their names is not recorded. One remembers that, as a result of the clan fight at Glenfruin, the Scottish king proscribed the name of Mac-Gregor and the clan, 'the nameless ones,' were scattered throughout Scotland—a dire punishment for a proud family.

Kite and Osprey in Flight

During a recent summer I happened to be near the nesting haunts of two of the rarest British birds, and to witness their departure in search of food.

The beauty and grace of the kite's flight have not been sufficiently appreciated. I was sitting on a grassy hill slope, the nesting territory of a pair of kites. The valley below me was made beautiful by woods of oak and birch: from the green hills came the passionate love songs of curlews, still vocal in late June. The kite rose from a thick grove far below me. She climbed in spirals, leaning on the west wind. Seeing, as I do, the golden eagle and buzzard in flight almost daily throughout the year, her flight was a revelation. She seemed light as thistledown. Her long reddish-brown tail, deeply forked, her wings, slender compared with those of buzzard or golden eagle, with white markings above, the effortless manner in which she climbed on aerial currents—all these things claimed attention.

The scene, too, was unusual for late June. Hawthorn trees in the valley and on the hillside were still in full blossom, and were loaded with snowy bloom. Above these snowy trees and bushes the kite climbed with delicate grace, with her wings not held stiffly like those of eagle and buzzard, but flexed at the elbows. When she was buffeted by the wind above a high grassy slope the kite dropped to where mountain sheep were grazing and then quartered the ground at the height of a man; but later, climbing to the cloud-filled sky, she became remote, intangible, and vanished from my sight. Her flight reminded me of no other bird of prey, except, perhaps, in some of her movements, of the hen harrier.

The osprey was seen in the country of loch and native Scots fir, where, thanks to the tireless efforts of the Royal Society for the Protection of Birds, a pair have successfully nested during the past ten years. It was a July day of warm sunshine, and I was walking through the forest, less than a mile from the osprey's nesting site.

Through my glass I saw what might have been a great black-backed gull leave the vicinity of the territorial tree. As the bird approached me I saw that it was the osprey setting out for a distant river to fish. It is usual for the bird to fly low and almost furtively on these occasions, but I now saw something different. The osprey began to climb in circles on the light breeze, as a golden eagle might do before setting course for its hunting grounds.

I was able to keep the bird in the field of my glass, and, at approximately 2,000 feet, it began a fast glide that would have taken it without effort down-wind to its fishing waters. The osprey's flight lacks the grace and buoyancy of the kite's, and the controlled power of the golden eagle's. Indeed, under certain conditions it recalls the figure of the great black-backed gull, and I wonder, on the rare occasions when ospreys have been shot by gamekeepers, whether they may not have been mistaken for that ruthless enemy of sheep and birds.

Now that we have several pairs of ospreys nesting in Scotland it might be advisable to issue a warning of the resemblance between the two species, for these two birds frequent the same rivers and lochs, and both prey on fish, the osprey habitually, and the great black-backed gull occasionally.

Northernmost Point of the Misty Isle

Hunish is the most northerly wing of Skye. Here the long swell from Arctic seas breaks in white spray against rocks of basalt, black as midnight, as greater black-back gulls on patrol call hoarsely. In winter in these northern latitudes the day is short and at four o'clock in the afternoon three golden flashes may be seen across the Minch to the north-west as the light on Eilean Glas on Scalpay, a few miles from Tarbert, Harris, is kindled.

Eilean Glas was the first lighthouse to be erected in the Outer Hebrides. This was as far back as 1789. A new tower was built in 1824, with a modern lantern and burner.

The second lighthouse to be established in the Outer Isles was the Uisinish Light, which stands on the rugged south-east coast of South Uist almost in the shadow of Corodal where Prince Charles Edward Stuart was concealed in a cave for three weeks before crossing to Skye in the care of Flora MacDonald. Uisinish Light shone for the first time in the year 1857. The lighthouses of the Isle of Skye were not established until a much later date.

Hunish looks out northwards to the high Shiant Isles, the home of sea birds and seals. In the strong and turbulent tidal streams which flow past and between these islands the supernatural Blue Men are said to swim with the seals. Here, in the summer dusk, in an atmosphere strange and fey, and when one is tossed in a small open boat on the great swells of the fast tidal stream beneath the grim precipices of these islands one realizes that their Gaelic name, na h-Eileanan Sianta, the Bespelled Isles, is an apt one.

So high are the Shiant Isles, the snow lies sometimes on their cones when the grass is green on their lower slopes: very beautiful are they of a winter morning when shortly after sunrise the snows glow pink while yet the green sea waters of the Minch are in shadow.

I knew one of the last of the human inhabitants of the Shiant Islands. She later lived in Uig, in that sheltered hollow between Portree and Duntuilm—an old lady of courtly manners, whose only language was the Gaelic. Her youth had been spent on the Bespelled Isles, where her father had been a shepherd.

The pair of sea eagles recorded by Martin Martin must have

lived, they and their descendants, on the Shiant Isles for centuries. It was about the time when the people left the island group that the eagles disappeared.

Hunish, like the Shiants, is now uninhabited, yet on the low grassy point beneath the hill the contours of lazybeds are clearly seen. The last to live here was a cailleach who gathered tangle seaweed and dried it on low stone walls for kelp: the walls remain as her memorial. The pasture is good, and Cheviot sheep graze here, heedless of the solans which pass frequently on their way to the Sound of Harris, thence to the Stacks of Boreray, nearly fifty miles beyond the Outer Hebrides.

North-east and east of Hunish rise the great hills of the Scottish mainland. Most distant is Foinne Bheinn of the Reay Forest, a long hill of attractive shape almost eighty miles away. Rather nearer, but still distant, are Cuinneag (the Milk Stoup), the noble dome of Suilven near Lochinver, and the lofty, splintered summits of An Teallach, above Dundonell. In aloof majesty rises the great hill of Slioch, its base in the cold waters of Loch Maree, its head often in cloud.

One morning of mid-December the view of these splendid hills was of exceptional beauty. So clear was the air that the snowy peaks rose like miniature Alps. The low, mid-winter sun cast their long shadows, and by three o'clock in the afternoon the primrose tint on the snows was changing to delicate rose. Even Farraval, which is no more than half the height of Foinne Bheinn, and even more distant, thrust its snowy head above the far sea horizon, in the neighbourhood of Cape Wrath, like a distant, sun-bathed cumulus cloud. Although Farraval looked its eighty miles from where I stood, Foinne Bheinn, almost as far away, seemed near in comparison.

I remember on Foinne Bheinn, a day almost equally clear, this time in summer. From that hill one can see North Rona, Sula Sgeir, and, to the north-east, Sule Skerry (where are a lighthouse and a meteorological station) and gannet-haunted Suleskerry Stack. I was lying on the high slope of Foinne Bheinn, 'spying', with my glass, at this stack, which was so thickly populated by the gannets as to be snow-white on the blue horizon, when a golden eagle soared, at a distance of perhaps three miles, into the field of my telescope.

In Skye south of Hunish and only a few miles distant, were the sharp peak of Sron Bjornal where, according to tradition, the Norse princess who married the first of the Martins of Bealach is buried, and the picturesque ruins of Duntuilm Castle. A younger son of a later

Martin of Bealach was Martin Martin who published the remarkable book, *Description of the Western Islands of Scotland* in 1703. The ruins of his father's house are still to be seen on the north-facing hill high above Duntuilm Castle.

Martin Martin was evidently an outstanding man. He is known to have been 'governor', or tutor, to Donald MacDonald, younger, of Sleat, he who later led the Sleat men at the Battle of Killiecrankie in 1689. From 1686 to 1692, Martin, who had graduated M.A. at Edinburgh University in 1681, was Governor at Dunvegan Castle to the young Laird of MacLeod. His standing is shown by the fact that he gave two addresses before the Royal Society on the customs of the Hebrides. His book, which was published about seventy years before Dr Samuel Johnson and his friend James Boswell made their celebrated Hebridean journey, inspired that expedition and was their faithful companion.

To the east of Sron Bjornal is Flodigarry with its pleasant trees, the home of Flora MacDonald for part of her married life. It may be recalled that the Jacobite heroine married young MacDonald of Kingsburgh, and that Johnson writes with enthusiasm of his visit to the pair.

Across the sea from Flodigarry the houses of Gairloch, now a thriving fishing port, are visible on a clear day, and each day after sunset six quick white flashes of light are seen as the lighthouse on Rudha Reidh kindles its lamp. South of Flodigarry are seen the islands of South Rona and its near neighbour Raasay. Raasay's highest hill, flat-topped Dùn Caan, is often thought, from various viewpoints, to be a part of Skye, yet the strait that divides it from Skye is of a remarkable depth. The latest Admiralty survey shows that the maximum depth of water here is 1,062 feet. This is deeper than any known part of the sea off the west and north-west coasts of Scotland, right out to the distant Continental Shelf.

I have said that the ruins of Duntuilm Castle can be seen from Hunish, at no great distance. This castle might well be mistaken for an ancient ruin, yet when first I knew the district the tradition was still clear of its windows brightly illuminated for a ball given by the MacDonalds of Sleat in 1730 in honour of Lord Lovat—presumably the Lovat who lost his head after the rising of 1745.

The stones of the high and substantial walls of the farm of Duntuilm were taken from the castle, and accelerated its ruinous state after it had been abandoned by the family because, according to one tradition, of its haunting by Donald Gorm, who died a barbarous death in the dungeon.

Each winter the surviving walls of Duntuilm Castle, built as they are on a most exposed promontory, are beset by tremendous gales, and are gradually but surely collapsing. Gone is the galley incised in the mortar of one of the low arches by a master hand—perhaps by one of the skilled craftsmen who built the arch, and traced it before the mortar hardened. The moat which guarded the castle on its landward side is almost filled in, but the almost impregnable sea gate is still visible.

This is close to the entrance of the filled-in dungeon, which in recent years has from time to time been partly excavated. An acquaintance of mine some years ago spent a summer night in its gloomy recess, in his quest for occult phenomena. He persuaded a neighbouring crofter to lend him his collie to help in the experiment. He said afterwards that the dog showed considerable signs of disquiet, but I wondered whether that uneasiness might not have been caused by dark, strange, and uncomfortable quarters in the companionship of a stranger.

Yet there are strange tales told here. For instance, from time to time a body of Highlanders have been seen to pass right through Duntuilm Lodge (it is now a hotel) as though it did not exist. A good many years ago, my wife and I were sitting at a window of the lodge with an old lady who 'had the sight'. Some distance away a girl was approaching the lodge—someone we knew well. Our companion turned to us excitedly. 'Who is that man following the girl?' she said in an agitated voice. There was no one, so far as we could see, but the old lady remained in a nervous and agitated state until the girl had reached the lodge and had entered the porch.

Place-names in the close neighbourhood of Duntuilm Castle recall dark deeds of the past. There is the Knoll of Justice, where the MacDonald Chief pronounced sentence on evil-doers and enemies, from which there was no appeal. Close to it is the Hangman's Knoll, where the gallows were erected. A rather higher hillock bears the name Cnoc Rolla, Knoll of the Rolling. It is said that those judged guilty of an offence were placed in a nail-studded barrel, which was then rolled down the steep slope. It is also said, with what truth I am unable to discover, that if they survived the experience they were liberated.

But to return to Hunish—its storms and glorious view. It is a Norse name—Hunn in old Norse is a bear—but it is generally thought to be, in this instance, a personal name. Skye, of course, was a Norse island until after the Battle of Largs in 1263, and a large proportion of the place-names are still Norse.

I recently discovered on Hunish a curiously shaped rock near the sky-line (see p. 24). As one passes this rock from a distance of 200 yards or less, it suddenly assumes the perfect form of a bear sitting on its haunches. It is not far from the rough track that leads down the cliff face to the old cultivated land on the low promontory, and many Norsemen must have seen it when they lived here.

The roads of Skye are thronged with cars during the summer months, but Hunish retains its aloofness, its quiet, and its dignity, with its bear of stone maintaining a ceaseless watch as it looks out over the sea towards Norway.

Mull of the Great Hills

The Island of Mull has the old Gaelic name Muile nam Mór Bheann, Mull of the Great Hills. This large and beautiful Hebridean island faces the same problems of a new age as the Isle of Skye but has the disadvantage, or some will say the advantage, of being farther away from the mainland. In earlier days its chief port was Tobermory. It is now Craignure, three-quarters of an hour by steamer from the crowded streets of Oban. When first I knew Mull there was no pier at Craignure. The steamer was the *Lochinvar*, sometimes the *Dirk* or the *Plover*. The latter was on one occasion shelled by a German submarine during the first world war as she was crossing the Minch, and as the shells were bursting above the deck an old lady sitting on deck refused to take shelter, but agreed to open her umbrella as a shield. At Craignure the steamer on the daily run from Oban to Tobermory was met by MacBrayne's red-painted ferry boat. There was no engine in the boat and the crew had to row her. The ferryman was a venerable bearded islander, by name Currie. Now, largely through the generosity of a distinguished son of Mull, a pier has been built at Craignure, and MacBrayne's mail steamer, a ship of over 2,000 tons, calls several times daily from Oban with passengers, freight, and many motor cars.

The visitor to the Isle of Mull who drives his car off the boat at Craignure and heads south, towards Lochbuie, or the Ross of Mull through Glen Mór, might form the impression during the first few miles that the island is more wooded than it actually is. At Ardura the small oaks in Glen Lussa have changed little since first I knew them more than fifty years ago. Beside the Lussa is the memorial cairn to Dugald MacPhail, the Mull Bard, whose song, *An t-Eilean Muileach*, 'the Isle of Mull', with its haunting dignified air is sung wherever the Gaelic language is spoken throughout the world. The memorial was erected with the stones of his own cottage. At Ardura the road forks and the traveller to Loch Scridain and the Ross of Mull and Iona beyond it drives west through Glen Mór, the Great Glen. This glen is now almost uninhabited. On Loch Sguaban, one of the lochs in the glen, are the ruins of a small castle where Eoghann a' Chin Bhig, Ewen of the Little Head, one of the Maclaines of

130

Lochbuie, had his fortress. Near the road at Tormore is a small inconspicuous moss-grown cairn in the heather. This cairn, which few persons have seen or indeed know of, is historic, for it marks the spot where the headless body of Ewen fell from his horse. Our hero during a clan fight was decapitated by the stroke from a claymore, and the tradition is that the headless body remained on his horse while it galloped in terror a distance of half a mile.

Glen Mór is a glen of song and of sombre memories. It crosses Mull and reaches the Western Ocean at Loch Scridain, an Atlantic sea loch. Here Ben Mór Mull rises to a height of 3,169 feet. It is a splendid viewpoint and I have more than once seen the coast and hills of Northern Ireland from it. To the north the Cuillin of Skye are clear, and on a very clear day Beinn Eadarra in the north of Skye can be identified through a gap in the Cuillin range. The Outer Hebrides, from Barra in the south to the hills of Lewis in the north, can also be seen. On the shoulder of Ben Mór is a hill-pass of great historic significance. Celtic scholars and historians agree that this hill-pass followed the boundary between the Celtic kingdom of Dalriada and the kingdom of the Picts. Near the head of the pass are two very old cairns. On the south slope is Carn Cùl ri Eireann, Cairn with the Back toward Ireland, and, farther north, Carn Cùl ri Alba, Cairn with the Back toward Scotland. It is possible that Saint Columba crossed this pass when, from Iona, he travelled to Inverness, where he converted and baptized King Brude, the Pictish king. During that journey, almost at its close, one of the saint's followers was attacked by what would at the present day be known as the Loch Ness Monster.

The pass looks down upon Pennycross on Loch Scridain. At Pennycross is the site of the herb garden of the Beatons or Bethunes, hereditary doctors to the Lords of the Isles, and later to other Highland chiefs also. A celebrated member of this learned and distinguished family was An -t Ollamh Muileach, the Mull Doctor. His sculptured gravestone may be seen on Iona. On our journey across Mull to Iona we heard at his home near Pennycross a distinguished piper, Duncan Lamont, play the old Pibroch, 'I got a Kiss of the King's Hand' in the summer sunshine. Duncan in 1940 lost his pipes at Dunkirk during the evacuation of the British force. It was remarkable that his pipes were later found and returned to him. It was pleasant to hear the Ceòl Mór or Great Music played on the shore of Loch Scridain as the sun glinted on the small waves, and a white, billowy mist contended with the sun on the slope of Glen Seilisdeir, Glen of the Yellow Iris, on the north side of the loch.

Oystercatchers were on the shore beside him. When I knew Mull in the old days there was little traffic on the roads as I used to see many of these cheerful birds brooding on their eggs. As long as the car continued to move they sat tight, just as buzzards still do on telegraph posts in the Isle of Skye, but during my last visit to Mull I did not see a single oystercatcher brooding—with the arrival of cars, buses, and lorries they may have moved to quieter stretches of the island's shores. Gone are the days when each motor car was recognized, and the driver of a horse-drawn vehicle viewed it with alarm, swiftly moving to avoid it. In those days, half a century and more ago, Gaelic was the language of all the older people, and of many of the children. On my recent visit I was speaking to Neil MacInnes of Fionnphort. He has what Duncan Ban Macintyre, the Gaelic poet, called 'the two tongues'. Neil knows the various districts of the Isle of Mull well, and when I asked him how many families he could name in which the children could answer a question put to them in Gaelic he thought awhile, then said, 'I can name only one family.' It was interesting to hear from him that in recent years several Dutch families have come to live in the Ross of Mull.

In Mull, as in Skye, large areas of glen and hill have been afforested. After winding round the head of Loch Scridain the road ascends Glen Seilisdeir. This formerly treeless glen, cold in sea mist when we passed through it, is being transformed by an extensive young coniferous forest. Glen Seilisdeir leads down to Loch nan Ceall, Loch of the Churches, on which is the historic island of Inchkenneth. On this isle is an ancient chapel and recumbent gravestones to chiefs and prelates, for in olden times Inchkenneth was a stepping stone and half-way house for the pilgrim to Iona. Here Dr Samuel Johnson and his friend Boswell stayed happily with Sir Allan Maclean of Duart who was living there at the time with his two daughters. The learned doctor has put it on record that on Inchkenneth he found 'no gross herdsman, or amphibious fisherman, but a gentleman and two ladies of high birth, polished manners, and elegant conversation'. It was from Inchkenneth that Johnson and Boswell, under the guidance of Sir Allan Maclean, sailed and rowed to Iona. It had been twelve years since their host had visited Iona and as Maclean of Duart, the ancestral owner of the island was recognized (it was now the property of the Duke of Argyll), he and his guests had a great welcome.

On the shore of Mull, opposite Inchkenneth, the high Gribun rocks rise impressively from the sea, and on this day of white, floating mist their grandeur was heightened. It is seldom that the plant lover sees *Silene acaulis* in flower from a main road, as we did at the Gribun rocks on this June day. At the head of Loch nan Ceall are old woods of deciduous trees. Here the air was scented with the perfume of wild hyacinths, which flower as late as mid-summer on Mull and Skye. The chiff-chaff sings in those woods, and on the stones of the small river the dipper sings his song.

From here it is a run of only a few minutes to the Sound of Mull, which separates the island from the mainland at Morvern. At the south entrance of the Sound of Mull stands Duart Castle, where Sir Charles Maclean of Duart, descendant of Samuel Johnson's host, combines with distinction the offices of Lord Lieutenant of Argyll, Chief Scout, and Chief of his clan. When I visited the castle in 1934 his grandfather, Sir Fitzroy Maclean, was in his 100th year, a man mentally alert, of great dignity, courtesy, and charm.

South Rona

Rising between Skye and the Scottish mainland, South Rona is separated from its larger neighbour Raasay by the narrow Sound of Rona, well known to mariners. It is an island rather less than five miles in length. Martin Martin in his classic, *The Western Islands of Scotland*, dismisses it shortly and writes, 'this little Isle is the most unequal and rocky piece of ground to be seen anywhere'.

Rona—the name here is from the Norse *Hrauney*, Rough Island—was part of the lands of MacLeod of Raasay who, with his people, suffered severely at the hands of the Government for the part they had taken in the Jacobite rising of 1745. Thus Rona and Raasay were closely linked, and the eldest son of the Laird of Raasay was commonly referred to by the courtesy title of 'Rona'.

We sailed out of Portree Bay in Skye on a fine morning of late summer and as we reached the open sea channel dividing Skye from Raasay felt the lift of the northerly swell. Recent soundings have shown that the depth here is, at one place, as great as 1,062 feet, a depth not found elsewhere off the west coast of Scotland until the far distant edge of the Continental Shelf is reached. Fulmars glided inquisitively about us, gannets patrolled high overhead in search of herring shoals, and a shearwater sped northwards low above the water.

We landed on Rona at the little harbour near the south end of the island, in a land-locked bay, Acarsaidh Mhór (the Great Anchorage) by name. Here a pleasant house stands near the shore and in sight of it is a planted wood of pines and larches. The house is in good repair, and it is not until one reaches it that one realizes it is no longer occupied. There is now no human life on Rona except at the northern tip of the island where the lighthouse crew live; their wives and families live in Portree.

At one time an excellent path must have linked this south community with the larger village farther north on Rona, built in the neighbourhood of a rather larger bay which, in early times, had a sinister reputation. Dean Monro, High Dean of the Isles, in 1549 described it as 'an haven for hieland galeys, and the same havein is quyed for fostering of thieves, ruggars, and reivers, till a nail upone the peilling and spulzeing of poure pepill'.

Morag the cairn terrier and Rain the spaniel between them caught and killed a rabbit, while buzzards mewed overhead. The rabbit was placed on a rock, to be collected on our return, but when, two hours later, we looked for it, the buzzards must have forestalled us, for it had vanished. White ling and white bell heather blossomed beside the track. We crossed a pass and found ourselves looking down on the channel between Rona and the mainland at Applecross, with the misty hills of Torridon beyond.

The track now crossed again to the west shore and descended to a bay where stood the deserted village. Waist-high bracken hid the path and through it one groped one's way. Blackberries were ripening against the walls of roofless houses, and a sign of earlier human occupation was a grassy slope yellow with ragwort.

We passed the church, now roofless like the other buildings, and climbed a grassy slope to a cluster of smaller houses, carefully and substantially built. They were perhaps built after the hard times which followed the 1745 rising, when a contemporary account tells us that Government troops landed here when the rising had been crushed and one of the soldiers ravished a blind girl.

Across the sea to the east clouds drifted across Ben Storr in Skye and at times veiled the tall pillar of rock known as the Old Man of Storr. Ling more than two feet high (so tall that it resembled Mediterranean heath) grew near the path: the terrain, being rocky and full of hollows, gives shelter from the ocean winds. The ground on Rona is very lightly grazed; during a three-hour walk we saw no sign of either sheep or cattle, or indeed of stock of any kind, and this added to the feeling of loneliness and desertion.*

We found a more cheerful atmosphere when on a neighbouring island, Fladday, the Flat Isle as it was long ago named by the Norsemen. Here a small community of three families lives, and the atmosphere and surroundings recall an island of the Outer Hebrides. Fladday receives its mail thrice weekly. Our arrival concided with that of the postman, who was ferried in a small rowing boat across the 100 yards of sea which separate Fladday from the neighbouring

* At the extreme north end of Rona is its lighthouse. The visitor's book shows that the first entry was made in 1857. The signature, clear and flowing, is that of the lighthouse-keeper SLESSOR. He records that he came to 'the new lighthouse' on Rona from SKERRYVORE light. It was fascinating to read the pages of signatures over a hundred years old. They are works of art compared to the recent pages of scrawled, almost illegible signatures.

island of Raasay. Johnson and Boswell stayed with MacLeod of Raasay and his family, and wrote enthusiastic accounts of the hospitality they had received.

Fladday has an attractive freshwater loch where water lilies, even at the end of August, continued to open their large white flowers. The collie dogs of Fladday gave us a respectful and even warm welcome, perhaps because they see few visitors. During our stay on Fladday the tide had ebbed and the postman was able to return on foot across a stone causeway that joins the island to Raasay at low water. After crossing to Raasay he finds no road until he has covered five miles over the moors to where he meets the mail van.

The north wind was increasing in strength. Near Pabbay we passed a common guillemot swimming with her half-grown young and on our voyage back to Skye we were escorted by fulmars, revelling in the long swell and fresh wind. A young kittiwake, perhaps a month fledged, kept us company for some time and we were interested to see a party of great skuas, for the species does not nest nearer than 100 miles from Rona—which, by the way, must not be confused with the Rona north of the Butt of Lewis, where is a nursery of the Atlantic seal.

An hour later we were in Portree, with queues in the shops, buses from Bournemouth, Bristol, and Ribblesdale setting down passengers, and private cars occupying every parking place in the village square.

Golden Eagles in the Sun

Birds sunbathe more often than is generally supposed. On a May day of cold wind and bright sunshine I watched a brooding eagle fly from the eyrie. For some time she sailed across her nesting rock, then alighted on a heather-covered pinnacle. The eyrie was exposed to the strong east wind and I expected the eagle to return quickly to her eggs or downy young. But on the spur where she had alighted she found, unlike her shaded and draughty eyrie, strong sunlight and complete shelter. After a cold night's vigil on the nest she evidently appreciated the morning sunshine and perhaps thought that relaxation was necessary. Slowly and gracefully she sank into the heather and then, with a sudden gesture, opened her great wings, resting them widespread on the warm heathery surface. Her head and neck were resting on the heather and as she sunbathed the only movement to be seen was when a wind eddy now and then ruffled the tips of her long primary wing feathers. For half an hour she rested thus; then, warmed and refreshed, she perhaps remembered her responsibilities, folded her wings, rose to her feet, and sprang into the air. She sailed swiftly down-wind to return and land lightly on the shaded nesting ledge where, after a moment's pause, she walked slowly to the eyrie and settled herself on it to continue her brooding.

A fortnight earlier, at the end of April, I was watching another golden eagle's eyrie. This time it was the male, on watch near the cliff top, who indulged in sunbathing. On this occasion also the wind was cold and when the sun shone out warmly the eagle, standing on the closely grazed grass, suddenly spread his wings as though about to fly. Instead, he sank, with wings still outspread, to the ground. As the eagle lay there feeling the grateful warmth there was a sudden movement and the tail also was spread wide. That sudden opening of the tail feathers reminded me of the spreading of a lady's fan. How long the bird would have remained thus is problematical. For three minutes the eagle remained motionless, but a cloud now obscured the sun. The eagle half-closed his tail, but continued to lie on the short grass with wings outspread. Then a raven appeared in the sky and at once dived at the eagle. Surely this was an undignified position for the king of birds to find himself in. The eagle, like an old gentleman rudely disturbed at his fireside, rose hastily to his feet and a series of attacks sent him into the air. He climbed in spirals, the raven in close attendance, until the pair had entered a cumulus cloud that hung motionless above the cliff at a height that I estimated at 4,500 feet.

The third occasion on which I watched a golden eagle sun-bathing was about three weeks after the eaglet had taken its first flight from the nest. Father, mother and child were on a broad, grassy platform where two small trees grew at the edge of a cliff. The eaglet was standing on short green grass. Perched on the rock a few feet from it was one of the parent eagles; the other stood at the roots of one of the trees. The eaglet was feeding on the remains of a rabbit; after satisfying its hunger it began vigorous exercises, running about on the grass and beating its wings violently. Besides its smaller size, the conspicuous white patch on the underside of each wing showed it to be a bird of the year. One of the parents walked across to the rabbit carcass and began to feed on it. Seeing this, the eaglet danced round its parent, yelping its desire to be fed. Its pleading was ignored. A little later one of the parent eagles took wing, but soon returned, and for more than an hour the family party enjoyed the warm sunshine. It was the young eagle who indulged in sunbathing on this occasion, spreading its wings wide and resting prostrate on the warm grass. The lengthening shadows cast by the evening sun had not reached the party when I left them and began a long walk home.

The only photograph, so far as I am aware, ever taken of a golden eagle sunbathing was by Niall Rankin. He was in a hide only a few yards from the eyrie at the time. I have studied golden eagles for the best part of seventy years, and the fact that I have witnessed sunbathing on only three or four occasions shows that it is far from common. I remember once seeing, through field-glasses, an eagle on a cliff top. The bird appeared to be dead, and it was a surprise to me when it rose to its feet; I remember my relief when it stood vigorous, erect and alert. It had been lying on the ground, exposing its plumage to the sun.

The Enchanted Bagpipe of Shona Beag

On a late summer morning, after a night of rain and thunder, the Atlantic was calm and the high hills were hidden in cloud. We stood in towards the land, and as we passed close to a beach of white sand were in a region that was fairy-like in its mysterious charm and beauty. Even the bird life here was different. We were escorted by a flock of a score of oystercatchers flying in V-shape formation (this itself was curious). As we steered, apparently straight for a rocky shore and disaster, a narrow channel suddenly opened. Into this our pilot confidently steered and we found ourselves gliding in the shade of oaks, birches and hazels. Midges flew out to us and made their presence felt; a black guillemot was so engrossed in his morning bath that he did not notice the intruder.

When last I had been in the district two brothers of the name of MacDougall lived in a small house on the shore. Their simple courtesy and their charm were memorable. They have gone beyond our vision and their house is a ruin. Herons were fishing in the shallows and green cormorants flew seawards in alarm.

The North Channel, through which we steered, separates Eilean Shona from the mainland. The tide was ebbing and there was not a foot of water to spare beneath our keel. Seaweed and cockles could be seen through the clear water. On the chimney of a ruined house a heron stood sentinel, without movement, apparently indifferent to our passing at half-speed with little noise. Here one felt in a world of seclusion, a world of grey sky and green grass and trees, sheltered from all the winds of ocean; the world of the slow-striding curlew, the black guillemot and the querulous buzzard.

It was more than thirty years since I had last been here, and as it was low water my friend and I had then crossed the North Channel on foot, sinking into glue-like mud in which cockles lay. In the centre of the channel we were, for a few steps, in sight of the distant Scuir of Eigg rising, remote and mystical, across the sea. Its steep, rocky slopes appeared like some phantom precipice, bathed in the light of the sinking sun. That vision remains, across the bridge of the passing years. Shona and Shona Beag, like Lewis and Harris, are actually one and the same island, although they are owned by different proprietors. On that occasion Shona Beag was our destination, a place of peace and old-world atmosphere.

In the house of its owner at that time, among the Raeburns and relics of Prince Charles Edward, we were shown an historic bagpipe. It was given by the last representative of the hereditary pipers to the MacDonalds of Clanranald before he emigrated to America. The family of Macintyres emigrated to America in 1790 from their home at Uldary near the head of the River Moidart, and gave to MacDonald of Kinlochmoidart, whom they considered to be their chief, their historic bagpipe for greater security. It had, they said, been played on the field of Bannockburn. On the chanter was an extra hole, below the last hole for the piper's fingers. This was made on the advice of a fairy, who said that with the elf-hole the chanter would play music the like of which had never been heard.

One of the last pupils of which there is a record as having studied at the MacCrimmon College in Skye was a Macintyre. Indeed one of the outstanding pibroch tunes still played at the present day was composed by John Macintyre, in the year 1745, when Prince Charles Edward Stuart landed in the west to claim the throne. Its name is, 'My King has Landed at Moidart'.

The North Channel leads into Loch Moidart, past Shona Beag and Inver Moidart. Here a road eighteen feet wide has been driven round the coast, and is bound to change the entire character of this until now remote district. Some who have been working on this new highway have been always employed in the whaling industry and now find themselves out of work, for no British firm can now compete against foreign whaling companies.

Abruptly the course of our boat was changed from south-east to west, and at once we came in sight of the ruined Clanranald stronghold of Castle Tirrim. As we passed it the sun broke through the clouds and flooded the old castle in a pool of light. Cattle lay on the sand on the low shore which, during an unusually high tide, is flooded. The castle, it is said, was set on fire as MacDonald of Clanranald was setting out for the Battle of Sheriffmuir and it has not been lived in since. The shell has withstood the ravages of wind, wave and tide and its size and importance are still evident.

As we stood near the old doorway, a pair of red-throated divers passed swiftly high overhead. As if in salute they suddenly called, and the air reverberated with their deep-toned quacking. Louder and still more loud the cries sounded, reminiscent of the guttural cries of courting fulmars. The surrounding hills acted as a sounding board and the volume of this unexpected music was remarkable. The calls ceased as abruptly as they had begun, and again there was silence over the venerable castle which had seen many changes, and was now about to witness a new era.

August Violets on the Cairngorms

High on Beinn a' Bhuird, one of the eastern Cairngorms, is a great snowfield, The Laird of Invercauld's Tablecloth. Throughout the summer months it is a prominent object from the main Deeside road as the traveller approaches Braemar. It sometimes remains unmelted throughout summer and autumn, as during the year in which I write (1970). This snow lies in the shelter of Coire an t-Sneachda, the Snowy Corrie which, in these changing times, has remained the undisturbed home of red deer and ptarmigan while bulldozed tracks for skiers scar some of its neighbours. Nearly 2,000 feet below the corrie the River Quoich flows through its glen towards the distant Atlantic before it joins the Dee, which flows in the opposite direction and enters the North Sea. In Glen Quoich is a splendid wood of natural Scots fir, some of the trees being several hundred years old. There are many open spaces between these trees and the old heather (ling) growing here is in distinguished bloom early in August.

It was a mid-July day when my friend and I climbed to the Snowy Corrie. We waded the ice-cold river and climbed near a clear burn that hurried in a series of small cascades from its birth-place in the snow far above. High above us we could see many red deer feeding in the corrie: as we watched them the sky darkened and clouds descended on Beinn a' Ghlo in Perthshire and the hills of Glen Shee. Rain began to fall, and a peal of thunder came from the Dee Valley at Invercauld. In the rain and gloom we were cheered by the sudden sight of *Silene acaulis*, its small red flowers covering the whole of a large stone. The snow in the corrie had earlier covered the plant, and had retarded its flowering by almost two months. As we climbed higher and approached the edge of the snow the grass, although it was past mid-summer, was still brown and apparently lifeless, but after a nine months' imprisonment beneath the snow the parsley fern (*Cryptogramma crispa*) was growing fresh green crinkled fronds. This local and rather uncommon mountain fern receives its name because its wrinkled leaves have the appearance of parsley.

Violets are associated with spring, or early summer, even on the

143

hills, but in this high corrie the violet plants had been under hard and deep snow cover until mid-summer, and were only now flowering. These violets of the high hills are small and pale blue, and hide themselves in the short, wiry grass. Here, near the roof of Scotland, a curtain of rain covered us: daylight faded and a thunder peal crashed overhead. The small burn, even at its source, was rising each minute and we thought of the river far below us, and the effect of the thunderstorm on its water, for it had to be forded on our return journey. The deer which had been feeding in the corrie earlier in the day had moved as we approached, but a half-grown calf had been left behind. It may have been asleep when the herd left and now, suddenly awakened and in a panic, passed us at speed, covering the uneven ground downhill in a series of leaps and bounds. This deer calf was well able to look after itself, but fawns when very young are sometimes abandoned by their parent. Once when sitting on a hill plateau I saw a hind arrive from the lower ground and cross the hill. I thought nothing more of this but half an hour later I imagined I felt a pressure against my side. I quickly dismissed this as being absurd, but when later I attempted to rise to my feet I found myself held fast by a considerable weight. Looking down, I saw a small red deer calf lying sound asleep on my mackintosh. Its mother had abandoned it and I was set a problem to know what to do with the small creature.

In the Snowy Corrie of Beinn a' Bhuird we saw later that day, still in torrential rain, a hen ptarmigan with her half-grown brood. The young birds had been sheltering under the boulders, and, accompanied by their mother, flew reluctantly only a short distance. Young ptarmigan have to be tough to survive on the high hills. One stormy day I remember seeing a young ptarmigan blown into a lochan by a fierce gust as it tried to fly across the water. I imagined that this was the end of the young bird's career, but my sympathy was wasted. Without hesitation the youngster swam 100 yards straight to the shore, landed, shook itself and disappeared in the shelter of a stony slope.

As we descended through the corrie we saw a pair of red grouse and their brood. It is an interesting and little-known fact that a cock ptarmigan usually leaves his mate for some weeks after the chicks hatch but a cock grouse remains with them, acting as a sentinel, and assisting his mate to guard the young. These young grouse were perhaps a month old and flew with their mother fast down the corrie. One young bird separated from the rest of the party, but the observant mother noticed almost at once that it had strayed. Without slackening her speed she made a quick turn, flew back uphill, and called to the chick. It rose at once and together they flew fast to join the rest of the family somewhere beneath us. Before we reached the glen 1,500 feet below we passed dwarf birch (*Betula nana*), growing in long heather, and crowberry (*Empetrum*) plants with many black berries. The river was rising fast and looked formidable. My friend, springing like a chamois from rock to rock, crossed with the loss of his mackintosh. I took, as I thought, the safer way, wading where the river widened. The current was strong and the river bed uneven: without the steadying support of a strong stick I might have found myself following the mackintosh seaward. On the farther bank we rested and saw Cairntoul and Beinn Bhrotain free themselves from the clouds, and watched the green upper slope and stony summit of Lochnagar to the south east light up as the sun reached them. High in the clear air a golden eagle was sailing, perhaps drying out his wings after the thunderstorm. As he rose still higher it was seen, through the field of a telescope, that two small birds had risen to attack the giant. Time after time they attacked the eagle. Their bravery was stimulating, and the fact that they were house-martins, far from their nesting eaves somewhere in the Dee valley, made the incident the more memorable.

Again the sky darkened to the north and heavy rain could be seen falling in the high corrie where the violets flowered. On the screes of Cairntoul cloud suddenly formed as the rainbearing north wind reached them. The golden eagle dislikes a wetting. He saw the approaching storm, half-closed his wings, and in a swift glide descended to the shelter of the old Scots firs.

Fulmar Colonists of Dunrobin Castle

Travellers by air from Inverness to Wick, Orkney and Shetland pass near and admire the distinguished outlines of Dunrobin Castle in Sutherland, standing on high ground near the sea. Most human dwellings are dwarfed when seen from a height, but the grandeur of Dunrobin is not lost, and is even increased. It appears strong and abiding as an isolated cliff, and the fulmar petrels which have recently colonized it may have been attracted by its rock-like appearance. On the Scottish mainland it is rare for fulmars to nest on a house, although not in Shetland.

It was an unusual experience to awake in the castle on a morning in August and to see a fulmar brooding its half-grown young on the window ledge. There was little wind on the days when I watched these birds of ocean, and they were therefore unable to soar and glide backwards and forwards across the walls of this historic castle as they do in breezy weather. Those guests at the castle who have bedrooms above tree level have the unique experience of hearing the harsh, urgent quacking cries of the parent fulmars instead of the usual voices of sparrow and starling. It is only in recent years that the fulmars have colonized Dunrobin Castle and there have been obstacles in the way of their successful breeding. When first they came, each bird laid its single white egg on a window ledge. As the ledge had a slight slope, the egg usually dropped off, or if it hatched successfully the young bird sooner or later fell to the ground. In order to prevent this, I suggested that ridges of cement, less than an inch high, should be made near the edge of the window ledge. This was done, but the fulmars did not approve. It appeared that the ridges impeded their arrival and take-off, and they abandoned the ledges which had ridges. On the ledges which remain as they were originally the birds still lay, but very few young birds are reared. Even in September the fulmars still patrol Dunrobin Castle, tirelessly, during daylight hours, and perhaps also at night, for the fulmar is active both by day and by night. They do not come in from the east sea as might be expected, but fly down the coast from the north-east, often a little way inland. They may come through the Pentland Firth, and it seems likely that their feeding grounds are in northern waters. Like the shearwater, the fulmar is known to undertake, as routine flights, journeys from nesting territory to feeding grounds of several hundred miles.

At Dunrobin, did they know it, they fly over a castle steeped in Scottish history. The traveller Pennant, who visited the castle in August, 1769, tells us in his works that he saw near Dunrobin the most northerly field of wheat grown in Scotland, and that it would ripen that year in mid-September. In Pennant's time the fulmars were not there to see the pleasant gardens where, we are told, in a seventeenth-century account, all kinds of fruits, flowers and herbs were grown, and 'abundance of good Saffron, tobacco and rosemary'. When they are brooding, the fulmars look down on the historic St John's Well, in the courtyard. This draw-well is unusually deep, and is now covered over. It is unexpected, also, to see fulmars flying over rose gardens and mulberry trees, and sometimes through the wafted spray of a fountain; it must be strange for them to hear, children of ocean as they are, the songs of thrush and blackbird, the crooning of doves, the chattering of jackdaws. This castle to which they return to brood the egg or nurse the nestling is very different from some oceanic island out of sight of land beyond which they fly tirelessly in search of food somewhere between Scotland and Iceland.

Their neighbours, too, are unusual. The swallows which glide past the castle and the cuckoo calling from the woods which here grow to the margin of the tide, would not be considered the fulmar's usual neighbours. The southward spread of the fulmars, which now encircles the whole of the British Isles, as a breeding species, is remarkable when it is remembered that the species lays only one egg, and that it tempts fortune by leaving, unguarded and without defence, its downy young for many hours at a time. I once saw an almost full-grown young greater black-backed gull disgorge, intact and fresh, a young fulmar about a week old which had been brought by its parent. The adult fulmar has few enemies, but is preyed on by some coast-nesting golden eagles. A pair of eagles which I watched some years ago fed their child almost exclusively on fulmar meat; the victims, although skilled fliers, were unsuspecting as they flew along the sea cliff near the eyrie, and were not difficult to strike down. It was soon after the fulmars had established themselves on the coast of Northumberland that I was walking near Dunstanburgh Castle with Lord Grey of Fallodon, a great statesman and bird lover. He was then losing his sight, and as we walked I was able to tell him what birds were passing along the coast. When I told him a fulmar was passing he said, 'I can visualize in my mind the other birds you tell me of, but when I had my sight the fulmar was unknown on this coast. It makes me realize afresh the handicap of blindness, for I am unable to form a picture of it in my mind.'

Bird Hibernation: Theory and Fact

Naturalists in olden days believed that certain individuals of certain species of birds hibernated. Then came a period which lasted until very recent years, when scientists poured scorn and ridicule on the theory, which they considered childish and unworthy. Now, as if to show science that it is not infallible, a bird has not only been observed during its hibernation, but has been weighed and had its temperature taken, and other records have also been made of it in that state.

More than 2,000 years ago the disappearance of certain species of birds from Europe at the approach of winter was a fascinating mystery to bird lovers. Aristotle (384–322 B.C.) knew more about birds than most people. He formed the opinion that birds did migrate, although he had a suspicion that certain species, or certain individuals of a species, might remain to hibernate at their summer haunts. It seems to have been considerably after Aristotle's day that the hibernation belief was most widely accepted, but by Gilbert White's time naturalists were beginning to discard the theory. White discussed the problem at length in letters to his friend Daines Barrington about the year 1771. Barrington did not believe that birds hibernated, but White was inclined to be sympathetic towards this long-established theory. On March 9, 1772, he wrote:

As a gentleman and myself were walking on November 4 in pursuit of natural knowledge we were surprised to see three house swallows gliding very swiftly by us. The morning was rather chilly, with the wind at north-west, but the tenor of the weather for some time before had been delicate, and the noons remarkably warm. From this incident, and from repeated accounts which I meet with, I am more and more inclined to believe that many of the swallow kind do not depart from this island, but lay themselves up in holes and caverns and do, insect-like and bat-like, come forth at mild times, and then retire again to their 'latebrae'.

Thomas Bewick, the celebrated Northumbrian naturalist and engraver, entered the controversy in 1797. He had asked John

Hunter, anatomist and surgeon, if the swallow's anatomy was unusual and Hunter had said that he could find nothing unusual in the bird's make-up. Bewick quoted a writer he names as Mr Klein, who stated that swallows assembled in numbers on the reeds at the edges of rivers, clinging to the stems until they broke with the weight, when the birds fell into the river. 'Their immersion,' he wrote, 'is preceded by a song or dirge which lasts for more than a quarter of an hour.' Bewick scornfully discarded this theory of swallows spending the winter under water, yet he admitted that certain swallows had been taken from the water and had survived.

In their quest for an answer to the problem of bird hibernation, these and other naturalists concentrated their observation on the swallow tribe, and on the cuckoo, for their appearance and disappearance were more obvious than those of other migratory birds. Of the cuckoo it was said as recently as 1908, 'He wakes up and buys his whistle' at the time of the Wareham Fair. Another legend was that once when a Yule Log was thrown on the iron dogs of an open fireplace the cry of 'cuckoo' burst from a bird that had been hibernating within the hollow log and who suddenly found it uncomfortably warm.

Richard Kearton, writing at the beginning of the present century, quoted instances of birds apparently hibernating. Yet he added that 'what seems to be a fatal piece of evidence against the theory is that young migratory birds arrive in spring in a fresh dress of feathers.'

It is, perhaps, strange that almost all modern naturalists have agreed that it is impossible for a bird to hibernate when warmblooded animals such as bats, hedgehogs and dormice do hibernate. In Madagascar there are shrew-like mammals called tenrecs that aestivate (sleep in summer) in order to avoid excessive dryness and heat, which would, perhaps, deprive them of their natural food.

It has recently been found possible to produce a state of suspended animation, analagous to hibernation, in the human being. Many people must have read of the amazing recovery of a young woman recently who had been struck on the head by a falling tree. For 169 days she remained unconscious, and at the beginning of that period she was kept alive by being 'frozen' to lessen the effects of high fever—her temperature was artificially lowered by ice some 20 degrees. Similar treatment has been used with success as a shock treatment in cases of insanity, and also with premature babies, for it is thought that lowering the temperature conserves the frail energies. A doctor working in the Outer Hebrides once came across a case of partial hibernation in an old man. This ancient went to bed when winter came and remained all the winter in a sort of coma, occasionally being given a drink of warm milk. A pleasant way, this, to pass the dark days of stormy winter, provided a devoted attendant is present!

Mammals which habitually hibernate store up fat which provides sufficient energy to maintain their metabolism at a reduced rate. Some of this fat is stored around the blood vessels, some on the sheets of tissue which keep the organs in place. When an animal hibernates it relinquishes its temperature-regulation system and for the time being becomes a cold-blooded creature like the frog, whose body is approximately the same temperature as the surrounding air or water. Even now, little is known of the functioning of a warm-blooded creature's 'thermostatic control'.

Now, after years of scorn poured on former believers in bird hibernation, an example of a bird hibernating has actually been discovered. The bird is a relation of the nightjar, named, because of its call note, whip-poor-will. One was found in a crevice of a cliff in the Colorado Desert in California in December 1946, by a well known American naturalist, Edmund Jaegar. In 1947 the cliff was visited almost at the same time, and again the whip-poor-will was found in hibernation in the crack. It was visited regularly during the next three months and was in so deep a sleep that it allowed itself to be handled without protest. It was weighed regularly and had its temperature taken. No heart beat could be detected by stethoscope and no mist of breathing could be discerned on a mirror. Successive readings of its body temperature showed that it was no higher than 66 degrees Fahrenheit, a drop of approximately 39 degrees below its normal temperature. The bird remained in the same position, apparently insensible and without food, for at least eighty-eight days, and probably longer. During six weeks it lost only one gram in weight. This exciting ornithological discovery was already known to the Hopi Indians: their name for the whip-poor-will is *holchko*, the sleeping one.

A bird has a better insulating layer against cold than a mammal: its fluffed-out feathers form a perfect air trap to prevent cold air from reaching the skin. It would, therefore, be interesting to know if Jaegar found his hibernating bird with its feathers fluffed out. In Britain David Lack's researches into the life history of the swift, recounted in his excellent book, *Swifts in a Tower*, show that nestling swifts can survive several days without food and that on occasion they lose their temperature-control at night and become torpid, their body temperature dropping from 102 degrees Fahrenheit to 70 degrees.

Is it possible that our swift is at times capable of hibernation, or at least of becoming dormant for considerable periods? How else can the following record of swifts in winter be explained? On the morning of November 12, 1923, we were walking at the edge of a birch forest at Aviemore in Inverness-shire. Snow had covered the ground for several days and there had also been hard frost. Overnight a mild wind from the south-west had spread in from the Atlantic, the morning was soft and balmy, and the snow was rapidly disappearing. As we traversed the edge of the birch wood we literally rubbed our eyes. There, hawking for insects above the leafless trees, was a pair of swifts.

It is usually suggested that late swifts are Scandinavian birds, but Scandinavia in mid-November is snow- and frost-bound. Even in Scotland there had been a severe wintry spell. These swifts may have been on migration and may have been compelled, a fortnight or three weeks before, to enter a cranny, like the whip-poor-will, and there become dormant. What would have happened to them had that exceptionally mild day not intervened? Would they have hibernated, or would they have died? Is it possible that they again entered their cranny before the chill of sunset, and did, indeed, hibernate? If the whip-poor-will (not a very remote relation of the swift) habitually hibernates, who is to say that the British swift is incapable of thus passing the winter, if its southward migration is retarded until too late?

Enchanted Loch of the Isle of Skye

On the north wing of the Isle of Skye is the small secluded loch named Loch Seunta, the Blessed or Enchanted Loch. It is entirely concealed from the road and is almost unknown except to the inhabitants of the immediate district. In old manuscripts of the seventeenth century, and also in Martin Martin's *Description of the Western Islands of Scotland*, printed in the year 1703, the virtue of this lochan is extolled. Hear what Martin Martin has to say about it, and more particularly about the well which is close to its outlet:

'The most celebrated Well in Skie, is Loch Siant Well. It is much frequented by Strangers, as well as by the Inhabitants of the Isle, who generally believe it to be a Specifick for several Diseases, such as Stitches, Head-aches, Stone, Consumptions, Megrim.

'Several of the common People oblige themselves by a Vow to come to this Well, and make the ordinary Touer about it, call'd Dessil, which is performed thus; they move thrice round the Well, and make the ordinary Touer about it proceeding Sunways from East to West and so on. This is done after drinking of the Water, and when one goes away from the Well, it's a never failing custom to leave some small offering on the Stone which covers the Well.

'There are nine Springs issuing out of the Hill above the Well and all of them pay the tribute of their Water to a Rivulet that falls from the Well. There is a little fresh water lake (Loch Siant) within ten yards of the said Well: it abounds with Trouts, but neither the Natives nor Strangers will ever presume to destroy any of them, such is the esteem they have for the Water.

'There is a small Coppice near to the Well, and there is none of the Natives dare venture to cut the least Branch of it, for fear of some signal Judgement to follow upon it.'

White sea mist drifted very slowly in from the Atlantic on the day when we visited the Enchanted Loch. In clear weather the view from here is wide and remarkable. South-east, east, and north-east, hill upon hill form the horizon. Ben Aliginn, Slioch, and

An Teallach, Suilven and Cuinneag; even Foinne Bheinn and Arcuil in the far-distant Reay Forest, rise in beauty. But on this windless day a magic mist lay upon land and sea. The Atlantic might have been itself a hill loch, for no wave broke upon the low shore and the view over the sea was limited to a few hundred yards.

Martin mentions that the sacred loch 'abounds with Trouts'. In an even earlier record, it is written that to this loch 'Mackdonald brought sevin fair trouts, the product of which now innumerable'. These trout were rising to a late autumn batch of flies. The water of the loch is of remarkable clearness and the floor is of fine sand. It almost seemed that the trout themselves felt the sanctity of the place and realized that they were safe from enemies here. The fish, in weight perhaps a quarter of a pound to half a pound, cruised slowly and unafraid backwards and forwards. Evidently the shag which we had seen swallowing, with difficulty, a young conger a few yards out to sea did none of its fishing in Loch Seunta.

The 'coppice' mentioned by Martin still covers the little hill that rises steeply to the south-west of the loch. The confident and strong autumn song of an invisible robin came from this hazel wood where several wood pigeons were sheltering and were perhaps feeding on small hazel nuts. The waters of one of the 'nine Springs' mentioned by Martin were sufficiently strong to disturb the quiet surface of the loch where they flowed into it.

We were as yet not in sight of the celebrated well. It is indeed not visible until one has crossed, on an old stone causeway, the stream issuing from the loch. This renowned well of virtue is still in use, but it is not covered by a stone as it was in Martin's day. On the threshold of November a red lychnis was still in flower here, and the deep blue flowers of a backward plant of milkwort provided a vivid touch of colour. There is a strong flow of clear water from the well, and this almost at once joins the stream from the loch.

The seventeenth-century manuscript mentions that there are in Skye 'three things of which this Isle makes its boast'. I have already written of the hallowed loch and its healing spring. 'As to the second thing, the water of the well, running over the Dulse (a species of seaweed) gives it yellow tincture which renders it pleasant to the taste.'

It was certainly unexpected to see a flock of at least twenty mallard drakes and ducks swimming on the open water of the Atlantic only a few yards from the estuary of the stream. It is not usual to see this duck on the open sea, on an exposed coast without creeks or bays. On being suddenly disturbed the mallard swam in a compact flock only a short distance seaward and then, as the two human figures remained quietly seated in their full view, approached once more and returned to their former station. Times change, and it may be that the reputation of the well is largely forgotten by the present generation of the natives of the district, but it would seem that at least the mallard find pleasant feeding where the sacred water from the hallowed loch spreads out through the seaweed. Here oystercatchers whistle shrilly and flocks of curlew almost touch the water's surface with their long bills as they travel south at this season of migration, and the wild swans as they pass awake the echoes among the hills.

Lochan of the Red-throated Diver

High on the hill country of a Hebridean island, on a small heather plateau, the lochan is invisible until the climber is standing only a few yards from its low banks. Its water, deeply peat-stained, is shallow. Ravens pass over it often and at times the golden eagle sails lazily high above it; in the distance is sometimes heard the mournful whistle of a golden plover. On the horizon are many hills and a sea loch of the Atlantic. It is a lonely country, this summer home of a pair of red-throated divers, which have laid their eggs and reared their young here for many years. On a summer evening in June I climbed to the lochan. Its water, after more than a month of sunshine, was very low. I looked across to the wee island on which the two large, dark, elongated eggs are usually laid. There was no diver on the island, nor was she swimming on the water. It was evident that the birds had that year deserted their ancestral summer home.

As I stood a few yards from the bank, thinking to myself that the abnormal lowness of the water had caused the birds to lay elsewhere, I heard, apparently coming from close beside me, an extraordinary cry. It was a long-drawn wail, of exceptional power, ending in a deep moan. This was a fantastic, eerie cry, and I stood rooted to the spot. A minute later the wail again rang out, pleading, deeply sorrowful—a cry of despair, it seemed to me. Again silence for perhaps a minute, then the agonized cry again was heard. The cries continued, at intervals of approximately one minute. I thought of two possible explanations. A solitary hiker had perhaps met with an accident and, wading in the lochan, had been trapped in the liquid peat. But, I reflected, the cry was too loud and shrill for any human distress call. After a time the cries ceased. I walked to the end of the lochan, satisfied myself that no diver was there, then walked back along the shore, to search for the human being, or perhaps a sheep, or lamb, in distress. Suddenly, to my amazement, I saw close to me, out on the lochan, the diver crouching motionless on her nesting cup on an islet I had never before seen appearing above the water's surface. It was pure peat, and entirely without plant life or indeed shelter of any kind. Its one advantage was that the brooding bird could dive in an instant into the water. It must be remembered that the true divers never take wing from the nest, but always dive, and swim submerged for some distance before they surface and show themselves.

It was indeed unusual that she had not dived when I had passed close to her. It is possible that she was a young bird and this was her first laying. Even more remarkable was her wild crying, as any species of bird sitting close rarely indeed gives away her nest by calling. My astonishment at seeing her so near was great, but I continued to walk as though I had not noticed her, for I knew that if she was disturbed, and left the lochan, she would probably not return to the eggs. Those disquieting, even blood-curdling cries of great power which I had heard were the diver's calls for her mate. He was almost certainly fishing in the sea 1,000 feet below and a couple of miles distant and, perhaps fortunately, did not hear her.

Since the red-throated diver and the black-throated diver both lay as near water as possible, their eggs are often swept away by a rise of water. On one occasion I found two eggs, containing well developed young birds, washed up on the shore of the lochan after long and heavy rain early in July. That small peat bank, only a few inches above the water, was most vulnerable, but the dry weather continued and the two eggs hatched successfully. I did not go near the lochan again until 29th July. It seemed without bird life, but after a time I saw a 'rise' which might have been made by a large trout. I knew that the trout in the lochan were very small, so I waited to see what would happen. After a minute or more a young diver, still in its brown-coloured down, surfaced, and later I saw one of the parents. I walked away from the lochan until only my head and shoulders were visible to the divers and was standing motionless watching them when suddenly I saw the diver's mate flying in from the sea. Concealment was impossible: I could do nothing but stand without movement, a most conspicuous object on the short heather. In less time than it takes to tell, I watched the diver rapidly lose height for his landing on the lochan. I made sure he would see me and sheer off in alarm, but without hesitation he dropped, legs down, with a splash on the water. It was a thrilling, unexpected moment. A long, thin fish, perhaps an eel, was hanging from his bill. This fish, and his legs held at full stretch downwards, gave a grotesque appearance to the flying fisherman. When the turbulence of the water caused by his powerful splash calmed I saw that the second young diver had appeared from its place of concealment among the reeds, and that both young birds showed excitement at the prospect of a square meal. They were then approximately three weeks old.

On the afternoon of 31st August they were still on the lochan, at least eight weeks after they had hatched. They were now well grown and nearly ready to make their first hazardous and all-important flight down to the sea. That afternoon the parent diver came in from the sea at almost the same time as on the first occasion. In his bill was a thick fish, perhaps a small rock cod, and this was fed to the young. For two months the chicks had been on the lochan, attended, when small, by one of the parents, but unguarded by them for the last three weeks. Ravens and herring gulls often flew over the lochan, but the young diver is ever on the alert, and submerges with scarcely a ripple at the appearance of a possible aerial enemy. When the chicks hatched, the buds of bell heather and ling had scarcely begun to form; now the south wind was fragrant with heather scent and the hills were purple.

On 31st August a strong south wind blew day and night, and also on the first day of September. On the afternoon of 1st September the young divers had gone. Perhaps that first flight was made during the short hours of darkness. Even the adult red-throated diver sometimes finds it difficult to 'take off' from a small lochan. When submerged it swims below the surface to the leeward end, then rises to the surface and 'taxis' against the breeze, using wings and feet until, like a flying-boat, it has reached a speed sufficient for it to become airborne. Indeed on a windless day it may remain quietly, almost submerged, on the water rather than attempt to fly. It must therefore be a hazardous and anxious task for the parent divers to persuade their young to leave the lochan for the first time. Should they land on the ground before reaching the sea there is no hope of their rising again, for a diver, because of the position of its legs, can walk only a few yards on land, and that with difficulty. For a young untried bird the whole operation must be indeed hazardous, and could not be carried out except in a strong breeze. The sea is the diver's true home and on the sea the young birds remain until they are mature and will themselves seek out a moorland lochan on which to nest. A diver cannot soar, but the flight when arriving at the lochan from the sea is fast and powerful. Indeed on one occasion the noise of its flight as it neared the lochan called to mind a jet plane at a distance.

Three species of diver are found in the British Isles, namely the great northern diver, the red-throated diver, and the black-throated diver. The largest is the great northern diver, which is a winter visitor from Iceland; it has never been proved to nest in Britain. (In the summer of 1970 there was a report, on reliable authority, that a pair of great northern divers had successfully bred on a Highland loch.) The black-throated diver nests on a comparatively large freshwater loch and finds most of its fish in that loch. The red-throated diver nests usually on a small hill loch and flies down to the sea to fish. All three species are, when in their summer plumage, extremely handsome birds.

MacCrimmon's Wall on Hasker

Perhaps the most celebrated pipers in Highland history were the MacCrimmons. At the summit of the hill called Glas Bheinn, rising from the sea strait which separates the Isle of Skye from the mainland near Glenelg, is a cairn called 'MacCrimmon's Cairn,' said to commemorate Donald Mór, one of the greatest composers, as he was one of the greatest players, of the MacCrimmon family. This I have described in another chapter on page 67.

The cairn on Glas Bheinn is remote and few pipers have visited it, or know its history. Even fewer have heard of MacCrimmon's Wall on the rocky island of Hasker. This island, named by the Norsemen Deep-sea Skerry, rises from the blue Atlantic some nine miles west of the machair and sands of North Uist. It has never been inhabited, and is one of the nurseries of the grey seal in the Hebrides.

Fifty years and more ago when I was in North Uist, I heard a strange story about Hasker. Long ago, a man who wished to be in complete seclusion asked the local fishermen if they would take him to Hasker and leave him there. It was a remarkable request, for there is no harbour or sheltered shore on Hasker and the great Atlantic swell almost continuously pounds it: a man on landing on it might be cut off for months from his fellows. The name of the stranger made the tradition more impressive and strange. I was told that the man was 'MacCrimmon'. Even in the Isle of Skye Mac-Crimmon is, and always has been, an unusual name, and all who carried that name were related, closely or distantly, with the great piping family. There were no MacCrimmons in North Uist, and because of this the name of the stranger was remembered clearly when I was told the story, which I have not seen in print.

MacCrimmon was taken across the ocean to Hasker and was put ashore on one of the few days when the Atlantic swell permits a landing on Hasker. It was autumn, and he was given food to last him through the winter months. The tradition was silent on whether MacCrimmon survived a winter on Hasker, but the ruins of a roughly constructed shelter are still seen on the island and bear the name MacCrimmon's Wall. Is it possible that the stranger was none

other than Donald Mór MacCrimmon? It may be remembered that after setting fire to the thatched houses of some of the Kintail men, Donald Mór for long was a fugitive, and on several occasions narrowly escaped death. After surviving many dangers he was befriended by the chief of the Mackays, and that great pibroch, 'Lament for Donald Duachal Mackay,' is probably his composition.

We will never know if MacCrimmon of Hasker was indeed the illustrious Donald Mór, but it seems almost certain that he had some connection with the great Skye pipers. Let us hope that a pibroch may one day be played beside MacCrimmon's Wall on Hasker by a celebrated piper of the present generation.

Hasker has sometimes been called Hasker nan Ron, Hasker of the Seals. On a day of sunshine in October, the Atlantic swell was at rest and I was able to make a landing on the island. October is the month when the grey seals gather and have their communal nursery where the rocks are lower, near the centre of the island. White-coated babies and angry mothers moaned dismay and defiance. A few of the more timid mothers slithered across the rocks and dived deep into the water but most of them remained on guard; their duty, even in the face of possible death, was to remain.

In a narrow sea channel, where the water was so deep that the bottom was invisible, two seals were asleep. In their sleep they 'surfaced' with closed eyes, took a deep breath, then submerged. One of the two dropped like a stone to the depths and indeed may have slept on the floor of the ocean. In seven minutes the great seal slowly appeared, like a human diver emerging from the depths, unhurriedly expelled the air from its lungs then, still asleep, once more disappeared from view into the green depths. MacCrimmon must often have seen this sight. If he had his bagpipe with him he may have played to the seals. I have, more than once, brought them close to me on a low ocean rock as I played. They swam close to me, unafraid.

The Flat Islands of the Ocean

In the Hebrides a number of isles have the name Fladday, which is of Norse origin and means Flat Island. The island lying far out in the Minch between Skye and the Outer Hebrides is named, because of its remoteness, Fladday Chuain, Fladday of the Ocean.

It has been uninhabited for a century and more. Barnacle geese have their winter home here: in summer a large colony of Arctic terns are often present.

Fladday Chuain has associations with the past. Here are the foundations of a chapel dedicated to St Columba, and near it is an ancient burial ground. About forty years ago burrowing rabbits unearthed here a human skull of exceptional size. A friend of mine who was then studying medicine and later became a well known surgeon was intrigued by this skull and wished to send it to Sir Arthur Keith, the celebrated anthropologist.

Perhaps wrongly, I dissuaded him, and the skull has now disintegrated. It was supposed to belong to the monk O'Gorgon, a man of exceptional stature and bearing (in the words of Dr Samuel Johnson), 'a tremendous name'.

Martin Martin, writing almost 270 years ago, records that a stone five feet high stood at each end of O'Gorgon's grave. There is now no trace of these stones, but for many years two upright stones of approximately the same height (one of them is still in position) stood on either side of the road on the neighbouring coast of Skye, two miles south of Duntuilm Castle.

I have often wondered if these are the two stones which originally marked the monk O'Gorgon's grave. On the day of our visit, a huge bull grey seal eyed us through the surf not far from this ancient burial place. The animal's head was dark red, and this gave the seal a strange and almost sinister appearance.

The tide ebbed, and the tangles swayed, half uncovered, in the northerly swell. Sea and sky were grey; the air was cold, as on a day in October, and the only colour was from flowers of sea thrift, still blossoming in the month of July.

As one stands on the high ground of Fladday Chuain, one sees that it is separated by a narrow strait from a group of smaller, bird-thronged islands to the south east. Most interesting among them is Bord Cruinn, the Round Table, which is sometimes named Mac-Donald's Table because of an incident in the first Jacobite rising in 1715.

It was on the flat, grassy top of this island that Sir Donald MacDonald of Sleat concealed his title deeds before leaving for the Braes of Mar to join that rising. Martin, when he wrote, perhaps twenty years before this rising, may well have been given a hint by Sir Donald of what might happen, for he recorded of MacDonald's Table:

'It has only one place that is accessible, and that only by one man at a time. One single man above the entry, without being expos'd to shot, is able with a staff in his hand, to keep off five hundred attaquers, for only one can climb the Rock, and that not without difficulty.'

The last time I did that climb, I found that a colony of storm petrels were being preyed upon by a neighbouring colony of greater black-backed gulls, and that the small, sooty wings of the small petrels had been stripped from the bodies, of which only the skeletons remained. The ruins of the small shieling in which the watchman had his home are still visible: it must have been a long and anxious vigil, but apparently the place of concealment was never suspected by those in authority.

In Martin's day a family had their home on Fladday Chuain, and it is unlikely that the shy barnacle geese wintered here, but the author mentions that a great flock of golden plover arrived here in September, and left again in April. These must have been the northern golden plover from Iceland, which still have the same habit. Martin writes:

I told the tenant he might have a couple of these at every meal during the winter and spring, but my notion seem'd very disagreeable to him: For he declared that he never once attempted to take any of them, tho' he might if he would. At the same time he told me, he wondered how I could imagine, that he would be so barbrous as to take the lives of such innocent creatures as came to him only for self-preservation.

The fulmar was not known on the Fladday Chuain island group in Martin's day, but there is now an increasing colony on Mac-Donald's Table, and these share the cliffs with kittiwakes and guillemots. The puffins nest on a smaller, grassy island. There is an old belief that the puffin flocks, when first they arrive from their oceanic winter quarters, make a turn sun-wise round the island, and that they do this also before their autumnal departure. In July it is usual to see gannets, singly or in little parties, moving swiftly towards their fishing banks. That year these skilled fishermen were scarce: perhaps because herrings had not appeared in any numbers in western waters.

During a southerly gale in the winter of 1962, a Swedish coaster in the blackness of a starless night and driving rain ran hard aground on the rocky coast of Fladday Chuain, and was so badly holed that she could not be refloated. There is now little left of her, and the island shore is piled with wood and debris. There were, at the time she struck, rumours that she was carrying a cargo of whisky and cigarettes, and the neighbouring coast of Skye, and also of the mainland, were hopefully searched. So far as I know, nothing was discovered, and there is now little left of the ship.

Hill Pass of Kintail

At the head of Loch Duich, a sea loch of distinction and charm in the West Highlands, a wild mountain pass leads across the high hills eastward. At the present day this pass is usually named Bealach an Sgairne, Pass of the Murmuring, perhaps because of the outcry of the winds near the summit. An earlier name for the pass was Cadha Duthac, Narrow Pass of Saint Duthac, commemorating the saint who is associated with Saint Duthac's Well at its crest. That was a thousand years ago but the church he founded still bears his name, for it is Clachan Duthach, Church of Saint Duthac. The church is in ruins, but its burial ground is revered and is still in use at the present day. The last wish of those who die at a distance from the Country of the MacRaes is often that their mortal remains should rest in the sanctified earth of Clachan Duthac. There is a Gaelic song of beauty and sadness that is sometimes played as a slow march on the Highland Pipe, 'I will return home to Kintail'. Loch Duich itself takes its name from Saint Duthac.

The entrance to Bealach an Sgairne is at Dorusduan, three miles north-east of Clachan Duthac where in July motherly eider ducks accompany young families on the salt water of the sea loch. When my companion and I, with faithful Rain the spaniel, left Dorusduan, we saw the dark clouds of the early morning rise from the hills as we approached the entrance to the pass, where a herd of wild goats is sometimes seen. Near Dorusduan we crossed the River Connag. There is a ford here which is associated with a tragedy of several hundred years ago. A celebrated Gaelic poet, Donnchadh nam Pios, Duncan of the Silver Cups, who was part-author of the historic Fernaig Manuscript, had returned from the east through the pass on his journey to his home in Kintail. The day was Friday and the river in flood. Now it happened that Duncan's servant had the fatal gift known as 'The Charm of Friday'. If, on a Friday, those who 'have the gift' should glance, even unwillingly, at one in danger while crossing a flooded river or stream, the result is fatal. Knowing this, the servant crossed first, and lay, face downwards, on the further bank. As his master failed to wade ashore beside him in the time he had expected, he lifted his head in his anxiety and looked towards the turbulent water. Even as his eye rested on the torrent, and on his master struggling against it, he saw him stumble, fail to regain his balance, and disappear in the dark rapids. A foot-bridge now spans the river here.

The grey mists were being roughly herded across the rocky face of Glas Bheinn, the Grey Hill, by a strong breeze from the north-west. The pass begins at the foot of Glen Connag, sometimes called Glen Choinneachan, and crosses several small streams. Beside gravelly springs the first flowers of the yellow saxifrage (*Saxifraga aizoides*) were opening. This saxifrage is fastidious in its habits. It must have gravel of red sandstone, and it must have clear running water, preferably ice-cold water from a spring near. Unlike most of the hill saxifrages its flowering season is prolonged through July and August, and sometimes even through September. A pair of grey wagtails, a bird that is becoming scarce in the Highlands, flew up the river, in graceful undulating flight. An hour's walk brought us to the mouth of a dark and splendid corrie in the great and rugged hill, Beinn Fhada, the Long Hill. Its name is sometimes given on the map as Ben Attow, which fails to give the sound of its Gaelic name. Below this corrie a formidable burn, swollen by recent rain, was not easy to cross. Here Rain the spaniel made an exciting leap across the strongest part of the stream, landing on a smooth rock considerably higher than the rock from which he had made his spring. We were now climbing more steeply, and slightly below us we saw an unusual sight.

Here was a spring so strong that when it burst from its dark source it was already a full-sized burn, and flowed in a series of short waterfalls to the parent river. A sudden shaft of brilliant sunshine lit up its waters and they became white as snow. In Iceland I had seen springs of equal volume, but in Scotland they are rare. We were now high on the Pass of Saint Duthac, or, if you will, Bealach an Sgairne. It may be compared with the Lairig Ghru Pass in the Cairngorms, but instead of Ben MacDhui and Braeriach rising on either side, the climber sees the high, rocky corries of Beinn Fhada to the south-west, and dark Glas Bheinn forming the opposite slope. The ground near the head of the pass was bright with Alpine flowers. Here, at the end of June, were luxuriant colonies of *Saxifraga hypnoides* in full blossom on the dry, inhospitable slopes which it loves. Near small, clear springs *Saxifraga stellaris*, the starry saxifrage, was in flower, its characteristic gold spots visible at the base of each white petal. The butterwort, which was already ripening its seeds in the glen below, was here in flower, and even in bud. In the screes were green fronds of the distinctive parsley fern. On the Cairngorms this fern grows at an elevation of 3,500 feet, but suffers from late and early frosts, for it is surprisingly sensitive.

Near the head of the pass is the well of ice-cold water, Saint Duthac's Spring, which during many centuries must have refreshed many weary travellers. One reaches the watershed and the head of the pass abruptly, and that sudden view eastward is most impressive. Five hundred feet below us lay Loch a' Bhealaich, Loch of the Pass, small waves sparkling as they reached its low, grassy shore. Even as we looked the sky cleared and the dark depths of the loch became blue and radiantly smiling. On the low island many rowan trees carried a mid-summer canopy of white flowers so thick that the old wind-harried trees seemed under a fall of snow.

High above us a fresh north-west wind drove white, fleecy clouds overhead; sun and shade rapidly alternated. On the east horizon rose the cone of Mam Sabhail rising to a height of 3,862 feet above the sea. In a local Gaelic saying this hill is referred to as 'Mam Sabhail of the Grass', because of the good grazing it provides. Near its summit a large winter snowfield was still lying. Near us wheatears flitted; a ptarmigan's egg, sucked and bleached, lay on the grass. The wind fell light; the air became still clearer. It was pleasant to sit on a grassy knoll on which the blue florets of milkwort contrasted with the green of club moss, a plant which is the badge of at least two clans, Munro and MacRae. The scene was lonely, beautiful, and remote, but as we sat an unknown visitor softly approached us. At an exclamation from my wife I turned my head and found myself looking into the eyes of a red deer hind not three feet away. There was no fear in those mild eyes, only friendliness and perhaps curiosity. Even when we stood on our feet the hind stood beside us unafraid; we heard afterwards that this hind had been hand-reared in the glen near Dorusduan and often followed the children home from school—but here she was four miles from the glen.

Here at Loch a' Bhealaich, high in the hills, is the quiet and placid source of a stream which, at the Falls of Glomach, is seen with admiration and respect as the second-highest waterfall in the British Isles. Like the Spey, swiftest of Scottish rivers, this young river for the first miles of its course flows as quietly and serenely as the Thames, unaware of the ordeal in store for it at the Falls of Glomach. A second, smaller loch, by name Loch Gaorsaig, is so near Loch a' Bhealaich that it appears as almost part of it. A third loch in the chain is very small: it has the curious Gaelic name Loch

Thuill Easaidh, Loch of the Waterfall Hole. Perhaps the name has a connection with the Falls of Glomach.

Beyond the strath we looked on the deep-green grassy slopes and stony summit of Sgùrr nan Ceathreamhnan (pronounced as Kerrinan), a distinguished and remote hill, its white rocks and boulders near the summit having the appearance of 'pockets' of newly fallen snow. The strath of Loch a' Bhealaich reminded me of Strath Dionard and Loch Dionard in Sutherland; there was the same remote mystical atmosphere and lonely beauty. That evening we turned and began our walk towards the west; when we reached the flooded burn we found that its volume was less and that the crossing was no longer hazardous, for we had first fortified ourselves with the mystic water of Saint Duthac's Well.

Perhaps 100 yards below the ford is a waterfall where sturdy rowan trees were growing; the scent of their flowers was warm and fragrant. One of these blossom-laden trees was so near the actual fall that the cold air of the cascade swayed its branches unceasingly and almost caressingly. That evening as we reached the foot of the glen and watched the sun set beyond the Hill of Silver we realized that here in the glen the flowering of the rowan was already over, and that clusters of berries were already being formed on the trees.

At ten o'clock that night the water of Loch Duich lay calm. The sun, low on the north-west horizon, still shone, and on the five sharp-pointed hills known as the Kintail Sisters, which guard the sea loch to the east, the rosy sun glow remained until twenty-five minutes past ten, when it set beyond the hills of Skye. Even at midnight there was little lessening of the light on that evening of mid-summer charm when the storms of winter were forgotten.

The Strange Fate of a Golden Eagle

On a September day of sunshine we had watched a pair of golden eagles on the high rocky coast of the Isle of Skye. The female had several times passed close to us, her great size and wide wing expanse making her an imposing object against the blue sky. Suddenly her mate appeared, coming in from the hills and as he approached he shot out his talons. The two great birds then played buoyantly and happily before flying together towards the grassy hill where they were accustomed to hunt rabbits.

It was six weeks later when we saw the male eagle, so changed in his appearance that at first we did not recognize him, or even his species. It was one of the few sunny days we had in Skye in October, and as we approached the eagles' territory we saw an eagle standing on a small rock on a grassy knoll, sun-bathing as we thought. We 'spied' the eagle through the glass, then cautiously and respectfully approached. Any moment we expected him to fly, but to our surprise he did not move. When he did he *walked* away, one wing drooping slightly as if injured. We now noticed that his plumage was unusually dark, more the colour of the sea eagle. Could this bird be one of the four young sea eagles which that summer had been brought by air to Scotland from Norway, where the race is still hunted, and had been reared and released a short time before by the Royal Society for the Protection of Birds, to re-introduce the race to Scotland if possible?

These young birds had been released when ready for flight on the island named Fair Isle which is south-east of Shetland and where there is a bird observatory. From Fair Isle to Skye is no great distance for an eagle to fly. We followed him over short heather and rough grass to the edge of the cliff, perhaps a quarter of a mile. We kept at a distance as he walked with partly spread wings; one wing was drooping, as though perhaps injured by an electric cable. He disappeared from view over a small rise, but when we had crossed this slope we saw him ahead of us. He was standing on a rock on the very edge of the cliff, the Atlantic 500 feet below. He looked at us without fear, and we were perplexed by the dark colour of his plumage; the golden head and neck, too, were dark. Through the glass, midges could be seen flying round his head. Quite apart from the injured wing this seemed a strange bird, quite unlike the eagle we had so often watched. We imagined that a sudden alarm would cause him to fall to his death, and did not approach nearer. Then a most remarkable thing happened. He made a sudden decision and literally sprang into the air. His injured wing miraculously recovered its full power, life and vigour returned to him, and he flew strongly perhaps seventy feet above the cliff for a distance of half a mile then, still flying well, he disappeared from our sight.

His behaviour was so strange that we telephoned to Fair Isle Observatory and spoke to Roy Dennis. We asked if one of their young sea eagles was missing. No, he said, their party of four was still with them. A fortnight later the calm of a Hebridean Sunday was broken by the urgent ringing of the telephone. A neighbour taking his Sunday walk near the coast had seen, below the small rabbit-haunted hill where the eagles were accustomed to hunt, an eagle sailing overhead, while a pair of grey crows dived at some object on the ground. He walked to investigate and to his surprise found a second eagle on the grass, unable to take wing. The bird had allowed him to lift it up and carry it home under his arm. It was light as the proverbial feather and was evidently starving. He asked us if we would come over and see the bird. We at once recognized the eagle as the bird we had recently watched, because of the dark plumage and the slightly drooping wing, on which one feather was partly displaced. There was no doubt about it—the bird was a male golden eagle.

The behaviour of this eagle, his strength ebbing and the power of flight gone, was impressive and memorable. He was quiet and dignified. With a royal gesture he raised the golden hackles on his neck and held them so. His eyes were clear, his expression was serene and intelligent. He turned his head slightly and looked quietly towards the sea cliff, thinking perhaps that he might see the dark form of his mate. His drooping wing and his tail were heavily impregnated with thin oil. This had dried, forming a coating like varnish, which had stiffened the joint on that wing so that it could not be flexed. His plumage was cleaned and dried but he was very weak and early next morning he died. Golden eagles and sea eagles at times prey on fulmars; when alarmed a fulmar often pours a stream of oil from its bill at the enemy. This seems to be the only possible explanation of the bird's fate. This happened several years ago and since then I have seen the female eagle, always alone, at the old nesting territory.

MacDougall Chief and the Robber

John MacDougall of MacDougall, Chief of the Clan, lived in the early eighteenth century. He was usually known as Iain Ciar, which may be translated in English as Dark-complexioned John. He was a leading figure in the first Jacobite rising in 1715, and on the suppression of that rising was an outlaw for a number of years. During his wanderings in disguise, he crossed the sea to Ireland in order to visit the Earl of Antrim, his kinsman. At the edge of a wide and dark forest, he was advised by a woman he met to continue his journey through open country, for she said that a noted robber lived in the forest, and waylaid anyone who should pass that way. She told Iain Ciar that so great a menace was the robber, the Earl of Antrim had offered a reward of £1,000 to anyone who should slay him and bring him his head.

The MacDougall chief, penniless and anxious to cross the sea to France to be beyond the reach of his enemies, thought that this was an opportunity not to be missed. He and his trusty companion, Livingstone by name, therefore entered the forest, and as they followed a faint and devious track through the dark undergrowth and beneath old and gnarled trees, it was not long before they saw the famous robber standing before them. He demanded from Iain Ciar his money or his life. The Highland chief was without more than the proverbial sixpence, but that was the last thing he wished the robber to know. Telling the highwayman that he was prepared to part with neither, he challenged him to mortal combat. Both men were expert swordsmen and the fight was long and hard, but the victory was at last gained by Iain Ciar, who carried the robber's head to the Earl of Antrim, and received from him the £1,000 reward.

The robber's whistle is one of the heirlooms at Dunollie Castle, Oban, the ancestral seat of the Chiefs of MacDougall, where the family still reside below the ancient stronghold on its rock looking out towards the Isle of Mull. Beneath the ivy-grown castle is an old and weather-beaten Scots fir. This tree is now upwards of 150 years old. It was planted to commemorate Captain Alexander MacDougall of MacDougall, of the 72nd Regiment (later the Seaforth Highlanders), eldest son of Patrick MacDougall, Chief of the Clan.

Captain Alexander was killed, at the age of 27, at Ciudad Rodrigo in Spain, in 1812. His miniature, by William Englehart, is preserved at Dunollie.

The name of Captain MacDougall is well known to pipers of the present day, for a celebrated composition in Ceòl Mór, the Great Music of the Highland bagpipe, was written in his honour by almost the last of the hereditary MacDougall pipers to the chiefs, Ronald MacDougall. The hereditary MacDougall pipers, while not so famous as the MacCrimmons of Skye, were players and composers of distinction, and the tune, 'Lament for Captain MacDougall,' is one of delicacy and feeling. These pipers lived at Moleigh, near Oban, and their portion of land was known as Croit nam Piobairean, the Pipers' Croft. Like the MacCrimmons, the MacDougalls had their College of Piping, the last who presided at this college being Ronald Bàn MacDougall, who was the grandfather of Ronald Mór, the last hereditary piper to the clan.

Four of Scotland's Most Confiding Birds

I think it is agreed by ornithologists that the most confiding bird in these islands is the dotterel; this bird must, therefore, come first on my list. For three other examples I have chosen another dweller on the high hills, the ptarmigan, and two birds much more accessible, the bullfinch and the robin. All who know and enjoy Len Howard's books must realize that the tit family are extraordinarily tame and intelligent, and they, too, must come high on any list.

The dotterel might be confused with the golden plover were it not for its smaller size. In the Highlands of Scotland it nests on hills between 3,000 feet and 4,000 feet, provided that the slopes are gentle and the ground is free of stones. Between the wars many pairs of dotterel had their nests robbed by collectors, for their richly marked eggs have made them eagerly sought after. During two days in June last year spent at the chief nesting haunt of the dotterel in Scotland I saw not a single bird.

I searched the hill where, some years ago, I spent many days in the company of a dotterel whose tameness, even for a dotterel, was outstanding. After the hen has laid her third egg she places them in charge of the cock bird. It is he who incubates them, and it is he who looks after the young brood. This particular bird had no fear of me, and I used to sit a foot or two from him as he brooded. All the same, he had his wits about him. I was careful to tell my collie to lie out of sight beside the cairn on the hilltop about seventy-five yards distant. Occasionally the collie, tired of this inactivity, would rise to her feet and take a few steps in my direction. At once the dotterel would rise and flutter away, as if wounded, over the ground; he obviously thought the collie was a fox. One day I saw the dotterel eyeing me expectantly. To my surprise and delight, he ran to me, picked a daddy-long-legs off my arm as I rested on the ground and, having swallowed it, looked into my eyes with a trustful expression before returning to the eggs.

One day when I arrived at the nest he was off feeding. A heavy hail shower came across on the strong west wind. The eggs of the dotterel are thin-shelled and can be cracked by hailstones, so I warmed and sheltered them. Then I saw the dotterel running

across the hill, and I had just enough time to replace the eggs in the nest before he arrived. He brooded the eggs at once with complete confidence, although I sat only a foot from the nest.

I have taken many photographs of dotterel, but I have yet to see the hen bird on the nest, after she has finished laying. She is larger than the male and has a more prominent white eye-stripe. That day the heat was tropical, and the hen bird I saw laying was so greatly distressed by it I brought a snowball from a neighbouring snowfield, placed it beside her, and saw her fall asleep.

The tamest ptarmigan I have ever seen was nesting on Braeriach, one of the Cairngorms, at an elevation of 3,000 feet. It had been an exceptionally snowy spring and the ptarmigan were still brooding eggs in early July. When a boy, I was told by a deerstalker of his feat in removing an egg from beneath a sitting ptarmigan without causing her to leave the nest. But my own ptarmigan was even tamer. She permitted me to lift her off the eggs and hold her in my hands. I then placed her in one hand and allowed her to remain there, at perfect liberty to take wing had she a mind to do so. When I replaced her on the eggs she at once brooded them. The next morning the young had hatched and the mother was brooding them a few yards from the nesting scrape.

On a day in early spring I once found a robin lying lifeless on deep snow high on the Cairngorms, across which it must have been flying on migration, for many Continental robins winter with us. The present generation of bird lovers know the late Viscount Grey of Fallodon only by name. Among the tamest of his birds in the grounds of Fallodon were the robins, but it was not until the last year of his life that he met a robin entirely without fear. This bird, having fed from the statesman's hand, did not fly off like the others, but daintily alighted on his hat, sang a song as if in thanks, and then flew away. The photograph that I took of it occupies a prominent place in the Edward Grey Institute of Field Ornithology at Oxford, which was founded to commemorate Lord Grey.

I have chosen the bullfinch as my fourth confiding bird because of the remarkable tameness of one bullfinch. She was so tame that she would perch on my hand and take hemp seeds held in my lips. She took as many as a dozen of these seeds at a time and was expert at shelling them. When she flew straight from my hand to the edge of the nest to feed her family, the young bullfinches had no fear of me. But if I came to the nest and there was no mother present to give them confidence, they were alarmed, and this alarm increased when they were feathered.

I think that the bullfinch taking seed from my lips and the dotterel picking a crane-fly off my sleeve were two of the most rewarding experiences I have had during a lifetime of bird-watching. Yet I sometimes wonder whether it is fair to a bird thus to win its confidence. For these feathered companions of man, especially the smaller birds, the world is a stern, merciless place. Cats and hawks wage relentless war on them, and when their mistrust and timidity are conquered by a human friend they may pay the penalty when that friend is not there to help.

Sunset in Skye

At last, after two months of wild, wet weather, the sun rose on a cloudless horizon. The sun at noon was warm—sparrows were carrying straw to their nests—and the air was so clear that I resolved to see sunset from high ground to the west of Quirang. I had made my decision rather late in the day, and it was necessary to climb quickly up a steep grassy face beyond the Storm Rocks, for it was after three o'clock and the sun was sinking towards the peninsula of Vaternish.

It was one of those rare winter afternoons, windless, and with exceptional visibility. The Minch lay entirely at rest, its water cream-coloured. On the Minch rose two island groups—the Ascribs and Fladday Chuain. On one of the Fladday Chuain group Sir Donald MacDonald of Sleat left his title-deeds for better security before setting out to join the Earl of Mar at Braemar before the first Jacobite rising in 1715.

About thirty years ago rabbits, burrowing in a very ancient burial ground on Fladday Chuain, unearthed the skull of a man of exceptional size. It was generally supposed to be the skull of the monk O'Gorgon, who is mentioned in old records.

Across the Minch rose Harris and North Uist. Around The Clisham, highest hill of the Outer Hebrides, thin cloud was drifting and Loch Seaforth, which itself seemed diaphanous as mist, wound deep into the hills where it formed the boundary between Lewis and Harris. As the sun approached the horizon the heather assumed a rich red-brown colour. I saw that every moment of time was valuable if I was to reach the hilltop before the moment of sunset. Actually I arrived there with two minutes to spare, and was able to 'spy' the Cuillin on the south horizon through my stalking glass.

Sun fires burned on the high slope of Bruach na Frithe, a hill which bears a striking resemblance to Mount Everest in miniature. The Cuillin were snowy, but the depth of snow on them was not great, and neither the hills of Trotternish, nor MacLeod's Tables in Duirinish, had snow upon them. At exactly two minutes to four o'clock the upper rim of the sun, glowing and pulsating, sank beneath the far horizon to the south-west. In the exceptionally clear atmospheric conditions I hoped that perhaps I might see the rare Green Ray at the moment of sunset. What I did in fact see was perhaps even more unusual.

At the instant the upper rim of the sun vanished a small area of brilliant vibrant blue held my attention. Then the light faded as if a cloud had suddenly formed, and the Cuillin became at once inky-blue.

Beyond them, and more to the west, rose Askival of Rum, on which is the highest shearwater colony in the British Isles. There was, this January afternoon, the bloom of a ripe grape on Askival. Two ravens sailed over, wings bent back as they glided to lower levels, but I did not see the small flock of white-winged snow buntings which had cheered me a few days earlier as they had risen almost at my feet.

Ten minutes after the sun had disappeared I saw, far across the Minch, three flashes of light as the lamp on Glas Eilean near Tarbet, Harris, was lit. Through a gap in the hills, eastward, a grey cloud seemed to float on the horizon. As I looked at it more carefully, I saw that it was the great hill of An Teallach, at the head of Loch Broom, dusk approaching its snowy ridges and summit. The moon, large and silvery, appeared above the Storm Rocks, and an hour after sunset the western sky was still full of colour.

The field-fares had come in to roost on the heathery ledges of the rocks, and the few rabbits which had escaped the scourge of myxomatosis were emerging from their burrows. The plague of field voles which attracted many kestrels and short-eared owls, has mysteriously vanished; one can now walk all day on the Skye moors without seeing a trace of vole or mouse.

Beneath me, lights appeared in the crofting township of Kilmuir. The name Kilmuir is from Cille Mhoire, Church of the Virgin Mary, a pre-Reformation name. The soil is rich and fertile; the enemy is the ocean wind. Two hundred years ago, the distinguished traveller Pennant named it 'the granary of Skye'. It was for centuries part of the lands of the MacDonalds of Sleat, and the MacLeods, casting envious eyes upon its rich soil, named it Duthaich na Stapag, Land of the Meal and Cream.

I looked down upon Monkstat, where Prince Charles Edward and Flora MacDonald landed that day of sea mist in the summer of 1746, and remembered that the fog was the means of preserving the Prince from the hostile MacLeods. The house of Monkstat is roofless, but the old ash trees, and remnants of a hawthorn hedge, remain to commemorate the MacDonalds of Sleat, who lived here after leaving their neighbouring castle of Duntuilm a few miles to the north.

On the High Cairngorms

It was pleasant, that summer morning, to see the old castle on Loch an Eilein in Rothiemurchus Forest and to think that the ospreys which nested there seventy years ago have, through the care of the Royal Society for the Protection of Birds, returned to the district. The loch was very low, and the heather dry and inflammable after weeks of drought. I had not been in Glen Eanaich for more years than I care to admit. The scene is now greatly changed; the bridges over the track were washed away by a cloudburst, and what was once the bothy by the Beanaidh River is now a heap of stones. Many summers ago I stayed a night here with a celebrated Dutch ornithologist, Professor J. G. van Oordt. The previous day I had shown him a dotterel's nest on a Cairngorm plateau nearly 4,000 feet above the sea. There was thick mist at the time and he was unable to take the photograph he wished. He had to go south by the morning train from Aviemore next day. At three o'clock next morning he set out on his long climb, and returned, successful, to the bothy in time to catch his train. I had first met the professor in Arctic Spitsbergen, where he was making observations on a king eider (a rare bird, even there) on her nest. He was a friendly man and showed the bird to an English bird-watching expedition who arrived in their chartered sealing sloop. The bird-hunters repaid his kindness by shooting the king eider on her eggs.

The Cairngorms carried much less snow than usual in late June, and the bell heather was already in full blossom in Glen Eanaich. The Beanaidh, flowing low and clear, sang a soft song, and with that song were mingled for a few minutes the notes of a piper's lament for one who had loved the Cairngorms and their birds. The sky was half-clouded and the air soft and fresh as we climbed through the ling heather. We looked across dark Loch Eanaich to the steep slopes and high rocks of Sgoran Dubh, and on the pleasant grassy corrie where in old days the people of Rothiemurchus had their summer shielings. We climbed by gravelly ridges where the last flowers of the creeping azalea, already going to seed, were pink. At a height of 3,600 feet we looked down on the blue waters of Loch

Coire an Lochain, which is Scotland's highest loch of any size, and saw a rising south-east wind send wavelets hurrying across it. In my book, *The Cairngorm Hills of Scotland,* I have recorded winter ice-floes still remaining on this loch in early July.

We were now approaching Scotland's highest plateau, and found its severity and Arctic character softened and beautified by the flower colonies of the cushion pink. Beneath the grey sky the dense clusters of red flowers, honey-scented, had attracted those strong fliers, bumble bees, to what is sometimes called the Roof of Scotland. The cushion pink is the only flower to thrive on the Cairngorms at 4,000 feet, and on the summit of Ben MacDhui flowers at an altitude of 4,300 feet above the sea. That was in the year of the exceptional summer when, as I have described in another chapter, the almost perpetual snowfield on Braeriach melted before autumn. The cloud layer thickened and the light became sombre; a cold wind came in gusts from the depths of the Garbh Choire to the south. This lessening of daylight reminded me of a very early morning one June in the 1920s, when my wife and I had climbed Braeriach to see the eclipse of the sun, and recorded the drop of temperature during that eclipse. Black-headed and common gulls now regularly visit even the highest reaches of the Cairngorms in summer, no doubt attracted by the food left by the many climbing parties, chiefly on the Cairngorm-Ben MacDhui plateau, to which the walker can now be transported by chair-lift. On this day the gulls passed over Braeriach plateau, sometimes flying low, then shooting skyward as a gust of wind caught them. The Wells of Dee were exceptionally low and it was strange to see scarcely a single snowfield remaining on the plateau. I find from my notes that one summer a snowdrift estimated at fifty feet in depth was, on 25th June, still lying above the young river where it plunges into the depths of the Garbh Choire; yet to-day, almost on the same date, there was no snow remaining here.

We crossed the plateau and looked into the stern depths of the Garbh Choire, the home of the great snowfield which remains unmelted almost always throughout summer and autumn. It was still extensive, but no larger than in the late July or early August of an average year. It was, as I record in another chapter, to disappear entirely that summer. The great height of the Braeriach plateau is impressive when the climber stands at the edge of the precipitous drop to the Garbh Choire and sees the Lairig Pass and the winding Dee at what seems an immense distance below—yet that low country is at least 2,000 feet above the sea. Near the Wells of Dee we were surprised to see a black-faced ewe and her well grown twin lambs; in Scotland a sheep at 4,000 feet is a rare sight.

We returned to Loch Eanaich by way of Coire Dhondail. The slope is steep and there is almost always at mid-summer the remains of a hard-packed and icy snowfield which necessitates caution. To-day there was no sign of snow, and the damp slopes of the corrie were a natural garden. Here the ground was literally carpeted with the white flowers of *Saxifraga stellaris*. I saw also the same variety or sub-species of *Pinguicula*, the butterwort, which I had seen on the Alps; it has a shorter and thicker stem, and larger and more deeply coloured blue flowers than the usual British species. The dwarf cudweed and Alpine sorrel were also thriving here. As we descended, it was noticed that at 3,000 feet above sea level the cushion pink had already formed seeds and was more than a fortnight earlier than the same species at the Wells of Dee.

One has many pleasant memories of Braeriach. There were clear summer days when the sharp peak of Faochag and the Kintail Sisters rose, intangible as clouds, on the far west horizon—when Ben Lawers seemed close at hand, and even Cruachan Beann, on distant Loch Etive of the Atlantic, was visible. There was one June morning when the grass was white with frost outside our small tent and as the sun rose it brought great heat, so that clouds formed below us and gradually rose to our high camp, bringing cold mist to replace glorious sunshine. Even more remote seem those memorable days when, an hour after midnight, the song of the snow-bunting greeted the dawn with loud, clear whistles that blended with the music of distant waterfalls. That evening in Glen Eanaich, a greenshank called from the topmost branch of a small fir near his feeding lochan, already, in late June, almost dry, though winter snowfields still lingered in high Coire an Lochain of Braeriach.